Acts of Salvation

Eight Plays for Advent and Passiontide

Kevin Yell

Resource Publications, Inc.
San Jose, California

Reprint Department
Resource Publications, Inc.
160 E. Virginia Street #290
San Jose, CA 95112-5876
(408) 286-8505 voice
(408) 287-8748 fax

Library of Congress Cataloging-in-Publication Data
Yell, Kevin, 1953–
   Acts of Salvation : eight plays for advent and passiontide / Kevin Yell.
      p.   cm.
   Includes bibliographical references.
   Contents: Glory be! — Celestrial secrets: the sequel to Glory be! — Paradise lost and found — A family Christmas tradition — No greater love — God of the outcasts — Come to my house — Weaving between heaven and earth.
   ISBN 0–89390–532–1
   1. Christian drama, American. I. Title.

PS3625.E45 A65 2001
813'.6—dc21

                                                                        2001041637

01 02 03 04 05 | 5 4 3 2 1

Editorial director: Nick Wagner
Production: Romina Saha
Copyeditors: Leah Faltus, Tricia Joerger
Cover design: Nelson Estarija

Contents

Acknowledgments

These plays were all written for the community of St. Paschal Baylon Parish, Oakland, California. They owe their genesis to the incredible support of the then-Pastor Father Robert Rien, who lived to regret (my words) his wonderful welcoming greeting when I arrived as a new pastoral associate: "Anything you want to do, the answer is 'yes.'"

While Father Robert was actually induced to be in one of the Passion plays and to "star" (as "MC1") in the original Advent play "Glory Be!", several choir members appeared in *all* these plays (*"what troopers!"*) and their director, Jenny Matteucci, was an absolute mainstay of each production. I was also completely dependent on the keyboard and musical skills of Daniel Lockert, especially when I wanted to change arrangements of popular numbers, adding instrumentation or vocal parts. Jenny and Daniel are a team that defies definition and creates beauty wherever it goes. Thanks also go to Sister Sharon Casey, OP, who acted as stage manager and production coordinator for most of the liturgies and, more importantly, the often thankless rehearsals.

The reading "Leaving Eden" (included in "Paradise Lost and Found") was created in 1991 as part of a preaching and storytelling course I took under Rev. Dr. Margie Brown at the Graduate Theological Union. I want to thank her for giving me and so many people permission to own our Scriptures, teaching us by example how to be humble in the presence of the Spirit in our lives and, even more especially, in the lives of others.

The final speech in "God of the Outcasts" ("Nilo Valerio is dead ...") is adapted, with permission, from "The Gift of Final Perseverance" by Father Edicio de la Torre. This piece is an actual eulogy given by Father de la Torre for his one-time seminary companion Nilo Valerio, who was killed by suspected members of the secret police in the Philippines during the Marcos regime. The reading is printed in *Celebrating One World*, published jointly by CAFOD (the Catholic Fund for Overseas Development) and The St. Thomas More Centre, both of London, England.

I want to thank the team at Resource Publications, Inc., especially Editor Nick Wagner and Events Coordinator Sue Espinosa. They have been wonderful enthusiasts for this work for several years, supporting the role of the arts in liturgy and catechesis. I am delighted that these plays will see America—and maybe beyond—thanks to them.

Because of copyright laws, we cannot print the music or words to the popular songs originally used for these services. However, references are made as fully as possible. If you have difficulty finding or performing the original songs used, deletions and substitutions can easily be made, according to local talent and availability of music.

These plays are dedicated to the Community of St. Paschal Baylon, who loved me into new ministry and deeper artistry, even if they did occasionally regret it.

Introduction

The tradition of using drama to teach and comment upon the salvation story—the Good News of Jesus the Christ—goes back more than a thousand years, to the *Quem queritis* trope of the Easter morning liturgy. A trio of clerics, carrying incense and candles, would walk from the sanctuary to an Easter garden somewhere in the church. They were accompanied by songs of the resurrection story and the visit of the three women to the empty tomb.

Not a great theatrical moment, you might say, and you would be right were it not for the fact that theater and dramatic representation had been all but eliminated from the Western world following the fall of the Roman empire in the fourth century. Until that time, anything theatrical would start with offerings to the Roman gods, which for Christians would have been an act of apostasy. Theater, therefore, was banned for Christians.

But the theater, along with all the other arts, grew in the dawning of the Middle Ages from simple beginnings and the natural yearnings of the human heart. By the end of the fourteenth century, every major religious center in Europe held dramatized liturgies and storytelling at different times of the year. In England, the Passion, Mystery, and Morality plays and cycles grew so large that they were sometimes given over by the cathedral chapter to the hands of the professional guilds (Goldsmiths, Tanners, etc.) to be produced, although always under the theological eye of the local ordinary or abbot. Plays or re-enactments told stories from the Bible and stories about Mary and the saints, or they moralized about Everyman. In them the stories of our history and the realities of the present came together in unique ways. To this day, groups are committed to producing some of these productions in modern as well as "historical" contexts, for example in Oberammergau (Germany) and York and Coventry (Great Britain).

The plays in this book were all written between 1995 and 1999 for St. Paschal Baylon Parish in Oakland, California, and they draw upon this long Christian tradition. The parish—the smallest geographically in the diocese— had the benefit of a supportive clergy, excellent music director, enthusiastic choir, and wonderful accompanists. They also had a not-too-large church building that had been renovated to allow for good sightlines to the central space and excellent sound for both word and song. Most importantly, the community, like those of the renaissance, welcomed the opportunity to create and share the stories that make us who we are, using all the arts at their disposal.

In the Mystery Cycles of Europe, we find both humor and pathos, the former chiefly reserved for the nativity stories, especially the scenes with the shepherds. It was not uncommon for contemporary people and events to be referenced in the plays, either formally or by improvisation. This tradition is continued in the present plays, particularly the Advent ones, and is to be encouraged in local performances. The contemporary theme is present in the Passion plays through costuming and by placing modern issues of social justice in the plays. Most particularly, the language and voice of all the plays should be that of the people, not proclaimed with overly pious tones or false "churchiness."

The issue of being "contemporary" is particularly pertinent for the musical choices, nearly all of which are from the popular repertoire. Music is a powerful way of spreading the Good News, and the pieces we chose brought extra power to the message of each play. Indeed, one extra benefit of doing the plays was that participants began to listen to radio and other musical outlets with new ears, looking for the "Good News" inherent in so many of the songs and lyrics around us. While the plays were first created with specific popular musical choices within the capabilities and talents of the local community, directors are free to change or delete pieces, swapping or adding new ones as the local talent and culture demand. Minor word changes and other suggestions are made throughout the plays. See also the "Music Suggestions and Sources" section for complete music references and other details.

Not everyone who wanted to be involved, including some in the parish choir, wanted to learn music by heart or be in costume. We therefore began a tradition of having an *ensemble* (originally called the "static choir," which was dropped when it became known, thanks to one wit, as the "stagnant choir"). While the *ensemble* was usually not in costume (often wearing just black), the members were always in full view and added greatly to the chorus singing and the community hymns.

As regards the script, sometimes Scripture is clearly quoted, and it is suggested that these words remain. Other words and speeches could be "translated" with regard to local culture, idioms, and colloquial phrases. Directors should feel free to make changes. Permanent staging was not used except for, on occasion, a large cross for the Passion play. Costuming was sometimes "historical," sometimes modern, and sometimes mixed, as noted in the individual texts. Movable risers and boxes were used at times for various scenes. Directions given in the text should be thought of only as suggestions and ignored where not helpful.

Most importantly, the plays were always given as part of seasonal liturgies, either as Advent carol services or as a Palm Sunday, Holy Week, or Good Friday liturgies in the evening. After the first year, we felt the need to repeat the services a second time, but always in a liturgy. Sample liturgies, which include the plays, are included for both Advent and Holy Week services. The first two Advent plays (the second a sequel to the first) were created as complete entities, with the prayers and hymns integral to the text. They were presided over by specific members of the cast.

It might also be interesting to know that the opening rehearsal was always just that—open to all. If there were too many people, we would just write extra parts or divide existing ones. While it was necessary to do some careful casting at times, directors should feel free to use the scripts as a basis for telling the story that needs to be told in your time and in your place, combining or dividing parts as necessary. Non-speaking parts, especially children's roles, can be added at will.

A major part of the experience of undertaking one of these types of plays is the spiritual growth that happens in the members of the cast. I always tried to contain rehearsals to the appropriate season (Advent or Lent) so that the meetings became a retreat for the participants, opening the story through personal participation. This active *Lectio Divina* frequently proved a powerful way of praying the Scriptures. Often the journeys undertaken by cast members were so powerful that the sharing of the dramas in worship with the wider community was just "the cherry on the top." They were worth all the work of preparing just for the personal growth they inspired in the cast members and the sense of community that was created as a result.

The Prologue

The Story of the Rainbow

One of the purposes of drama is to encourage people to look behind the scenes of our lives and explore the "what if" of pertinent questions. Through drama we can propose ideas, play out potential outcomes, and maybe, in the end and in our real lives, make more informed choices.

One question that we as adults often need to re-learn from the children in our lives is "why?" Why did Jesus have to be born? Why did Jesus have to die? Why is the rainbow all those colors? Why do you love me? The following script was originally created for the closing liturgy of a year-long sabbatical program at the Jesuit School of Theology in Berkeley, California— a year full of living in and exploring the questions of our lives.

Since then it has been used for the opening of Easter Vigils (especially in Cycle B) and other services. It is offered as a simple model of what this book is all about. "What if ... ?"

Reading: Genesis 9:12–15 (adapted)

READER   God said, "Here is the sign of the Covenant I make between myself and you and every living creature with you for all generations. I will set my bow in the clouds, and it shall be a sign of the Covenant between me and the earth. When I gather the clouds over the earth and the bow appears in the clouds, I will remember the Covenant between myself and the earth. And so the waters shall never again become a flood to destroy all life. When the bow is in the clouds, I shall see it and remember my everlasting Covenant with you."

Two Angels are at separate places, each with telephones. Angel 2 is holding a telephone. The other phone rings and is picked up by Angel 1.

1   Hello, this is Angel Celeste here, Storekeeper for the Department of Divine Signs and Wonders. How may I help you today?
2   Hello Celeste, this is Archangel Raphael here. God sent out an order to stop the rain and put out the rainbow a few thoughts ago, and I was wondering what the problem was. The rain stopped, I see, but there is still no rainbow. Is there a problem?
1   Well, I've looked everywhere in the storeroom, and we haven't got one.
2   Are you sure you haven't lost it?
1   I'm sure. In fact, no one here can even remember God making a rainbow in the first place.
2   But that's ... Actually, come to think of it, I can't remember God making one before either.
1   So I was just wondering ...

2   No way! I can't just go up to God and say, "You forgot to make the rainbow." God created for six days, then rested. After that, it was up to the world to get on with it, co-creators of the promise.

1   Well, that's it then. I don't know what I can do. If God didn't make one in the first place …

2   But we have to do something; God needs a symbol of the Covenant.

1   Well, maybe there's something else we could use that's already been made?

2   Hey! That's it! *We'll* make a rainbow! And we'll use six colors to remind God of the six days of creation. Then God will remember all the work that went into creating the world and won't destroy it.

1   Great! There's only one thing: How do we start?

2   Well, we'll just follow the model God used. Now, what did God start with?

1   Chaos.

2   Well, after the last forty days we certainly know all about that, don't we? What happened next?

1   The Spirit hovered over water—well, we've already got the rain.

2   And God created light. Great, so the rainbow will appear when the sun comes out in the rain! And we'll start with yellow for the sun because it's bright and speaks of new life.

1   Then came the vault to separate the waters, so let's have blue for the sea and sky.

2   And for imagination and inspiration.

1   Pardon?

2   Indulge me. I've been taking a poetry class.

1   The third day was all the vegetation on the earth, so let's bring in green for that.

2   That's a good idea. And next how about a deep, rich indigo for the nighttime stars to twinkle in. The color of dreams and shadows.

1   That's a bit romantic, isn't it?

2   Well, what's wrong with a bit of poetry in a symbol?

1   Nothing. I suppose some people might like it.

2   Besides, I happen to know God has a soft spot for poets. Anyway, back to this rainbow. Birds and fish came next.

1   Let's have orange for them.

2   Why orange? Most of them look dirty brown to me.

1   Look, if you can have indigo for—

2   All right! All right, Celeste. You let me have indigo for day four, so you can have orange for day five.

1   Thank you, Raphael. And then we can have red for the blood and passion in all living creatures for day six, and we're done!

2   Great! I think that'll look pretty neat. God will see the rainbow, remember all that was created in the six days, and stop the rain again.

1   I've just realized; it'll never work.

2   Why? A moment ago—

1   Yes, I know, but God made everything in those six days. So God could see the symbols of those six creations and just as easily think, "Why not destroy it all and start again."

2   So what are we going to do?

1   Put something in that God didn't make!

2   What are you getting at?

1   You said it yourself at the beginning.

2   Did I? What?

1   You said, "God created for six days, and then God rested. After that, it's up to them to get on with being co-creators."

2   Right! So you're saying we have to remind God of something good that humanity has created which God could not replace exactly because it was created out of human free will.

1   That's right, something like purple or violet, a mix of blue and red, water and blood, feminine and masculine. The color of regal power and repentance.

2   Now who's getting a little poetic?

1   Even Storeroom Keepers have their moments.

2   Fine with me. And besides, that's what I call a Covenant; six of God and one of the other. That's a deal worth making. I've got a feeling this just might fly! And who knows where it might lead?

1   Okay, you tell Gabriel to put the trumpet away, and I'll get the sun out.

2   Celeste, thank you; it was fun creating with you.

1   My pleasure, Raphael, and likewise.

They replace the telephones and hold a tableau.

READER   And God said, "When the bow is in the clouds, I shall see it and remember the lasting Covenant between myself and every living creature of every kind that is found upon the earth. Never again will I destroy life, but it shall live and prosper."

At that the sun shone forth, and the rainbow appeared. The earth breathed a sigh of relief, and God looked at the rainbow in the sky and saw what had been made.

And God's laughter split the clouds and God said, "Now that's good!"

Advent Plays

"Glory Be!"
(or "Angels on the Chorus Line")

A Celebration of Advent:
Yesterday, Today, and Tomorrow

When I first decided to write an Advent play rather than a Christmas pageant, I had to ask myself what Advent was all about, not just historically, but for today, and even for tomorrow. The answer seemed to be summed up in the word "annunciation," each one leading to that final one for "the end of the world." And I realized that it was angels who were always the bringers of the message. As mentioned in the introduction to this book, the nativity scenes of the medieval plays were also the place for humor and, literally, playing. Music and dance were used, as were occasional mention of contemporary people and events. The telling of this happy story through a counter-point of farcical and serious moments helped to keep the people's attention and opened them to the power of the message. Literary historians might easily see the origins of Monty Python or Saturday Night Live–style skits interspersed within the more traditional scenes and story-line of some of the medieval scripts. It is this playfulness that we are trying to find in this play and its sequel.

CAST
MC1, 2, and 3 (These are the lead angels, the Masters and Mistresses of Ceremony; they are the liturgical Presiders. They should represent the diversity of the community.)

A1–10 (These are the angels who speak. Parts can be further divided or combined as the numbers demand. Please note that several players share the words of what is traditionally one angel. This was a deliberate attempt to stop over-identification with one face per part.)

Historical Characters (These can be played by angels or others.)
    ABRAHAM (ABE) and SARAH
    ZECHARIAH and ELIZABETH
    JOSEPH and MARY

The CHOIR DIRECTOR (Needs to be able to lead the CAST musically and sing solo. They might be dressed appropriately, maybe operatically or with choir robes.)

The NON-SINGER (Might be a musical dude or just someone playing the part. They might be dressed as an historical figure, such as Einstein, Elvis, or Eleanor Roosevelt.)

The DANCER (and a dance team, if you have one)
  Accompaniment: minimum (keyboard(s) and solo trumpet)

The "plot" of the evening is a sharing of the fact that angels are continuously announcing parts of the salvation story, and they will continue doing so until they announce that final act, the end of the world. As such, these angels need to be rehearsed and generally kept on their toes. The telling of the three biblical birth stories is counter-pointed with the music and dance rehearsals that keep the angels ready. Those who know the show or movie *A Chorus Line* will recognize the format. Also, please note that a form of storytelling is used here in which the historical characters both say their lines and tell the narrative. This may take some getting used to, but it allows for the characters to "come alive" a little more without inventing (too many) words for them that are extra-biblical. It also allows for them to face the audience a lot.

For costumes, I asked all the angels to wear whatever they wanted, as long as it was white. (They could use silver and gold for trim and decoration.) The MCs should be the most flamboyantly dressed. We had white tie and tails for MC1 (a ring-master style), a very grand *My Fair Lady* outfit for MC2, and a wonderful punk angel look, with lots of silver chains and spiked hair, for MC3. The "regular" angels wore a mix of night clothes (with teddy bear), sweat suits (with "Gab's Gym" on the back in gold sequins), tennis outfits, ball gowns, and even one in an artist's smock complete with paint palette. Halos, wings, and feather boas were optional, while the ensemble, also in white, had their music in matching white folders. The accompanist arrived as Liberace, complete with a white tux trimmed in Christmas lights.

The set is very plain, as befits the Advent season, with maybe some risers on which the cast and ensemble can sit.

White feathers tied to pieces of silver or gold thread are placed in each and every service aid or handed out at the beginning.

Apart from the opening hymn (when *all* the cast is out of sight) the angels join the assembly for the carols, sharing the people's worship aids, and, if necessary, pushing their way into the middle of rows by walking along the pews to get to people in the middle.

Opening Community Hymn

Enter MC1, MC2, MC3 through assembly.

MC1   Ladies and Gentlemen, Children of all ages, welcome to a little bit of heaven! No, you've not died; you have been admitted, for one evening only, to that place where we of the angelic community and you of the earth can meet. What you might call a spiritual version of Oakland International Airport. *(Insert appropriate local venue.)*
        We heard you were celebrating the Advent story and thought we would come and share with you what it's about, at least as it's understood by us, the Gabriel Division of the Holy Angel Flying Corps.

MC3   Yes, "Gabriel's the name, annunciations are our game!"

MC2   Excuse him! That's right, we are Gabriel! Well, you didn't think *one* angel could do all that work alone, did you? No, there are lots of us, each ready in a unique way to be just the sort of Gabriel God needs in any situation.

MC3   And when we say "unique," we are not joking! Actually, you may not realize this, but every time God needs an angel for an annunciation, we have to audition! I mean, even after all these years on the job! Mind you, that is how we keep up our high standards.

MC2   Several of the angels who were not working tonight wanted to come to join you and share their stories. So please welcome "The Gabriels"!

All Angels enter from the back and sides, singing "One" from A Chorus Line, including Ensemble. We suggest changing the word "he" or "she" to "we," with appropriate other changes. Sing as much of the song as you need to move through the assembly, greeting people. End with a big Broadway-style tableau, maybe with a short kick-line at the front. At end of song, all sit apart from MC1, 2, and 3. If necessary, those playing ABRAHAM and SARAH exit to change costume.

MC2   Thank you! As we were saying, Advent, as we all know, is a time of waiting, waiting for something special to happen. And that something special is, of course, yes, you've guessed it … the end of the world!

MC3   Oh, you thought it was the birth of Jesus? No, I'm sorry, you can't wait for that, it's already happened! Didn't you know?

MC2   Of course they know, they go to St. ……'s! (*Insert name of church.*) Advent is the time when Christians look back to the first coming of the Messiah in history, but they do it to help prepare themselves for that future important event, the second coming of the Messiah, otherwise known as the end of the world.

MC3   So are you saying that the way these people look forward is to look back?

MC2   Yes, how else can a human learn to deal with what's in the future if they don't learn from the past?

MC3   True!

MC1   Which is exactly why we have come here tonight, to lead you on a journey into the past, into the annunciations of yesterday, so that we can all enjoy the one Big One still to come, when everything and everyone on earth and in heaven will, together, sing a song to welcome the Messiah again.

"The Hills of Tomorrow" by Stephen Sondheim, from Merrily We Roll Along, *can be sung by the whole CAST in a choir formation. Music may be used by everyone.*

MC1   The first annunciation was recorded back in the Book of Genesis and was made to Abraham and Sarah (*They enter*). You might remember, they were both well past retirement age when God called on them to pack up and start traveling to a new land. Because of the faith they placed in God (*Angels 1, 2, and 3 move out of their choir places and into position.*) and because they trusted that God's vision could be made possible through them, three of us—

MC3   (*interrupting*)   Three's a very popular number up here.

MC2   (*continuing*)   Three of us were chosen to appear to them at a place called Mamre, in the Promised Land. This is the story of that first annunciation.

ABE   It was the hottest time of the day, and Abraham was sitting by the entrance to the tent …

SARAH   … while Sarah was inside.

ABE   Abraham looked up and saw what he took to be three men approaching …

A1   … although they were really angels.

MC3   To really see angels, you have to understand, would have surprised him too much, especially at his age, and, of course, it would not have been correct for him to talk to women he didn't know, so God graciously observed the convention and let him see men. Just thought you'd like to know!

ABE   The tradition of hospitality demanded that Abraham should make the strangers welcome, so, jumping up, he invited them first to cool themselves by washing and then asked their permission to have a meal prepared for them.

A2   This they gave, for to refuse …

A3   … would have been impolite.

MC3   Besides, they were hungry. (*MC1 and 2 look shocked at interruption.*) Well, they could have been!

SARAH   So Sarah, who had stayed inside the tent, again as local custom demanded, began baking …

ABE   … and Abraham and a servant began preparing a young calf from the herd for the surprise dinner guests.

SARAH   It's a good thing they weren't in a hurry.

Music up, under dialogue: "The Hills of Tomorrow"

A1   After the meal …

A2   … the visitors asked Abraham …

A3   … Where is your wife, Sarah?

ABE   She's in the tent.

A1   I shall visit you again …

A2   … at the same time next year …

A3   … and she will then have a son.

SARAH   What? (*laughing*) At my age, there is to be such joy?

MC3   I need to remind you that although Abraham saw three men, they were really three angels, and angels are really just messengers of God. Got it? So when they spoke, it was really God speaking, and when Sarah laughed, God heard her and said:

A1   Why …

A2   … did Sarah …

A3   … laugh?

SARAH   I didn't laugh, honestly!

A1   And God said:

A2–3   Oh yes you did! (*Angels 1, 2, and 3 exit.*)

Music: "Hills of Tomorrow" transitions into introduction for "I Watch You Sleeping" by John Denver. Sarah picks up a "baby" from the "tent."

SARAH   And so, at the appointed time, Sarah conceived and bore a son to Abraham in their old age, just as God had promised. And they named him Isaac, which means "Laughter," for both of them had seen the joy that the news and the birth of their son had brought them.

SARAH and ABRAHAM sing "I Watch You Sleeping."

During instrumental section, the following is said:

ABE   Their son Isaac was in turn to have a son Jacob, who was also called "Israel" by the family. This Jacob was to become the father of twelve sons, each of whom would give his name to a whole tribe. And so the promise made to Abraham and to Sarah was fulfilled, for through Isaac they did indeed become the founders of a great nation.

Song ends. SARAH and ABRAHAM exit.

MC3   Some of you might be wondering what the requirements are to be an angel. Well, in the Gabriel Division, we set a very high standard, as you can see. Every one of us has been specially chosen for our communication skills. That doesn't actually mean we've got many of them; it just means God liked the ones we've got and thought they would fit the job.

MC2   Annunciations are very important events, and our boss, the Archangel Gabriel, has us practice in between engagements. And if you're thinking that we haven't done any announcing since the first Christmas, well, you're very much mistaken.

MC1   We cover every birth and death, in every language and nation. We attend marriage announcements, carry love letters, and even help out at civil events, provided they comply with the wisdom of God. Unfortunately, this last category has been particularly quiet of late. However, we are currently getting a surprising number of calls to attend small group meetings in certain churches and find this very encouraging.

MC3   Singing is very important for angels, but just to prove anything is possible to God, who can make angels out of anyone, we thought you would like to know the story of at least one angel who felt inadequate in this gift department.

The CHOIR DIRECTOR steps forward to lead the CAST in a couple of scales and arpeggios. The NON-SINGER enters from somewhere in the church, joining in.

CHOIR DIRECTOR (*stopping the CAST after a couple of painful interruptions from The NON-SINGER*)   Stop! (*to NON-SINGER*) Try (*sings*) la, la, la, la, la (*NON-SINGER does, painfully*)

The CHOIR DIRECTOR and the NON-SINGER sing, as duet, "Sing" from A Chorus Line. *All join in the scales at the end. Possibly add an "Amen" in the last measure of music.*

The CHOIR DIRECTOR and the NON-SINGER join the CAST.

MC3   To prove that God has a sense of humor, not being able to sing might actually be considered particularly appropriate for our next story, the annunciation of John the Baptist. (*looks of confusion from rest of CAST, especially MC1 and MC3*) Well, after all, he was the one who was to start crying in the desert! (*groan*)

MC1   God had, through the prophets, led the descendants of Abraham and Sarah to expect a Messiah. But such an event, the actual coming to earth of the Messiah, would need not only an angelic annunciation but also an awful lot of human preparation. (*Enter ELIZABETH and ZECHARIAH.*) A second Elijah was needed to bring about a spiritual conversion by the rest of the community. And that sort of work is technically outside our job description. We took, therefore, special delight in our annunciations to Elizabeth and Zechariah, for it was as if, in the person of John the Baptizer, we were announcing the birth of one of ourselves in human form. This is his story. (*ZECHARIAH establishes a "Temple" place, ELIZABETH is "at home."*)

ZECHARIAH   Zechariah was a priest. He was married …

ELIZABETH   … to a woman named Elizabeth, who could trace her family tree back to the priestly family of Aaron himself. But the couple was childless and getting on in years. (*Enter A3 and A4.*)

ZECHARIAH   It was Zechariah's turn to serve for a period at the Temple and, for one day only, his solemn duty was to offer incense in the inner sanctuary, in the Holy of Holies. There appeared to him an angel, the sight of which disturbed Zechariah and he was overcome with fear.

MC3   You see, I told you people were afraid of angels. I can't think why!

A3   Zechariah, do not be afraid.

A4   Your prayers have been heard.

A3   You and your wife Elizabeth …

A4   … are to have a child and you …

A3   … must name him "John"—

MC3 (*interrupting*)   which means "God is gracious."

A4   He will be your joy and delight, and many will rejoice at his birth, for he will be great in the sight of God.

A3   With the power and spirit of Elijah, he will go before the Lord to turn the hearts of parents back to their children …

A4   … and the disobedient back to the wisdom that the virtuous have, …

A3   … preparing a people fit …

A4   … to receive the Lord.

ZECHARIAH   How can I be sure of this? I'm an old man and my wife is … getting on.

MC3 (*getting into the scene and interrupting A3 and A4*) (*to ZECHARIAH*) Excuse me? This is an angel you're talking to! You're not meant to question us! (*to A3 and A4*) Do something! Don't let him get away with it. I know. (*to ZECHARIAH*) "Since you have not believed my words, which will come true at their appointed time, you will be silenced and have no power of speech until all I have said has happened." That'll fix him!

ELIZABETH When Zechariah came out to give a blessing to the people, they were amazed that he was dumb. By making signs, he made them understand that he had seen a vision in the sanctuary and was now unable to speak. When his term of service had finished, he went home to Elizabeth (*He does so.*) and shared with her all that had happened. And in due course, despite her age, Elizabeth conceived and was exceedingly joyful. She gave birth to a boy and named him John. When relatives complained, as relatives sometimes do, that "John" was not a family name, Zechariah asked for a slate and wrote on it: "His name is John." And at that moment his lips were unsealed and he praised God with these words:

ZECHARIAH Alleluia! Blessed be the God of Israel.

Community Song "Blessed be the God of Israel" [*Tune suggestion:* FOREST GREEN]

CAST join assembly for hymn. On the way back to their choir area, they call to DANCER to tell his/her story about how s/he became an angel. S/he needs a lot of encouragement. This can be ad libbed a lot. If DANCER cannot both sing and dance, another might either sing or dance.

DANCER Hello, er, well, this is my story, and they said I had to tell you about it. When you first become an angel, you have to go for an interview with God. And I mean, it's okay really, it just was a bit scary to think about.

Anyway, you go into this big room and it looks like a big cloud and this angel says not to worry and that everyone passes, but God wants to know what you do.

Well, I wasn't ready for that because I thought God already knew all about me. And the angel said: "That's true, but God likes to hear it from you. If you had your biggest wishes come true, who would you be for God, and what would you most want to do?" So I stepped to the middle of the room and coughed and started.

"Let Me Dance for You" from A Chorus Line. *Use as much or as little of the song as can successfully be choreographed in your space.*

MC1 And so we come to the most famous annunciations of them all: the ones to Mary and Joseph. For a long time, God had dreamt of the day when the rift between heaven and earth could be healed and he could once again come and walk with friends in the cool of the day. And so angels were sent out to find two people: a woman who would let the Word of God make a home in her body and a man who would let the woman make a home in his house.

Music up: "One" from A Chorus Line

MC2 So the angels flew over all the land (*The CAST do so, wandering throughout the church, "seeking."*) that had been given to the descendants of Abraham and Sarah. They visited the homes of all the faithful Hebrews, seeking out people who would welcome the Good News of a coming Messiah.

MC3 Actually, we even flew over a few other places too. There was this great couple in what is now Pakistan; then there was a woman in Ethiopia, but the nearest partner for her was in Uganda. Anyway, God decided that it was getting a little too complicated, and for the moment at least, we should stay in Israel. So—

MC2 And so, (*a little angry at being interrupted again*) when we came to a little town in Galilee called Nazareth, we found the special couple for whom God was looking. (*MARY and JOSEPH enter from opposite sides and CAST begin to find them. MARY and JOSEPH do not look at each other until place mentioned below. Half of CAST go to each as they sing.*)

"One" from A Chorus Line. *Each half of the CAST sing "Her" or "Him" versions as appropriate to either MARY or JOSEPH. Just use first verse. Rest of CAST then form a semi-circle around the couple (who are back to back) while Angels 5, 6, and 7 face MARY and Angels 8, 9, and 10 face JOSEPH.*

A5   Hail Mary, full of grace, the Lord is with you!
MARY   Pardon?
A5,6,7   Hail Mary, full of grace, the Lord is with you!
MARY   Oh!
A8   Hail Joseph, son of David, do not be afraid.
JOSEPH   Pardon?
A8,9,10   Hail Joseph, son of David, do not be afraid!
JOSEPH   Oh!
A7   Mary, do not be afraid, you have been blessed by God.
A6   Listen! You are to conceive and bear a son …
A5   … and you are to name him Jesus.
A10   Joseph, the one to whom you are betrothed …
A9   … is to bear a child through the power of God's Holy Spirit …
A8   … so you are not to abandon her but take her into your house.
MARY and JOSEPH (*together, still back to back*)   But how can this come about since …
MARY   … I am …
JOSEPH   … she is …
MARY and JOSEPH   … a virgin?
A5,8   The Holy Spirit will over-shadow you/her …
A6,9   … and the power of God will flow through you/her …
A7,10   … and God will make of him a Savior for the people of Israel.

MARY and JOSEPH turn and look at each other and then turn back to the angels and say:

MARY   I am a servant of the Lord. Let what you have promised come to be.
JOSEPH   Well, if it's all right with her, then I suppose it's all right with me!

Angels all raise their hands in blessing and slowly go back to their places during the following speeches and before next song.

MC1   And so Joseph took Mary into his house, and they cared for each other as husband and wife. And all the time, the child grew in her womb and they waited, like you today, for the event that would change the world as they knew it, the birth of the Son of God.

MC2   Now of course, being good Jewish people, both Mary and Joseph knew their Scriptures. Those stories of hope and expectation from the past were spinning in their minds and in their dreams.

MC1   They knew the story of Sarah and Abraham and Isaac. They knew the prophesies of Isaiah and the pain of their people, living in the shadow of oppression and fear. Would their Jesus really be a new David? Would he really restore a king to the throne of Israel? Or would their faith and hope be foolish? Only God knew and only time would tell.

MARY and JOSEPH sing "[I Don't Know Much] But I Know I Love You" by Linda Ronstadt and Arron Neville.

Community Song [Suggestion: A setting of the Magnificat]

MC3   Well, that sort of brings us up to date, really. I mean, there were lots of other annunciations to do, of course. There was one to the shepherds and, of course, the three to the wise folk from the East. They did the annunciation to Herod, which was not such a good idea, but there again, you can't limit annunciations just to the people you want to know. The shepherds, of course, told everyone in the inn next to the stable, and the inn-keeper's wife told the story to her family every year at tax-gathering time. And so it has continued, down through the ages, until it comes to you. Each generation has told the stories, adding bits and forgetting others.

MC2   Which is where we came in. What are you waiting for this Advent? Who is the Christ that wishes to be born in you this Christmas? And how will that help you to prepare to celebrate the end of the world?

MC1   Because, like it or not, that's what we are all warming up for, our very last annunciation, the coming of the full and total reign of God, the day when all those who have been journeying back to Eden for all these centuries will be welcomed home. The Abrahams and Sarahs, the Elizabeths and Zechariahs, the Marys and Josephs of all of history. On that day, Gabriel will blow the trumpet like it was going out of style. I can hardly wait!

"Blow, Gabriel, Blow" by Cole Porter from Anything Goes. *Suggest it is led by one singer (maybe CHOIR DIRECTOR) and then whole CAST joins in. Choreographed as fully as CAST are able.*

MC2   The time is coming for us to depart and to send you back into the world. But before we go, we thought we would give you all an opportunity to try out as angels for some future careers. Each of you should have received a small piece of angel power on the way in. (*CAST all hold up and wave their feathers on threads, previously hidden on their costumes.*) We invite you to hold onto that now so that you can all be commissioned to be earthly angels for this coming season and spread this Good News, not just of the birth of Jesus once upon a time in Bethlehem but of the birth of Christ in human hearts and lives this very Christmas.

MC3   So heavenly angels, are you ready?

ANGELS   Yes!

MC3   And earthly angels, are you ready?

ASSEMBLY   Yes! (*Repeat, with gesture if necessary.*)

MC3   So let's stand and let's go! And the answer is "Amen!"

MC1   Angels of Earth and Angels of Heaven, do you believe that the God of All is in love with the universe? If so, please answer Amen!

ALL   Amen!

MC2   Angels of Earth and Angels of Heaven, do you believe that Christ will return to bring life and to save? If so, please answer Amen!

ALL   Amen!

MC3   Angels of Earth and Angels of Heaven, do you believe that all are called to bring forth the Christ in their hearts and their lives? If so, please answer Amen!

ALL   Amen!

MC1   In the name of God the Most High …

MC2   In the name of the Source of all Life …

MC3   In the name of all Goodness and Truth …

MC1,2,3   Amen! Alleluia! Amen!

MC1   Be commissioned as Angels of Good News and Hope …

MC2   … to bring comfort and joy to a world caught in fear …

MC3   … and bring laughter and tears to a world needing both …

MC1,2,3   Amen! Alleluia! Amen!

MC1   Be brightness and light, be friend to the stranger.

MC2   Be a "Gabriel" to all who need one.

MC3   Be happy; don't worry, and let all the angels say:
ALL   Amen! Alleluia! Amen!

Community Song "Glory Be" [*Words: Kevin Yell; Tune:* ODE TO JOY]

1.   "Glory be to God in heaven and on earth be peace to all!
     Glory in the highest heaven!" Hear the angels' Christmas call.
     God to earth will soon descend and peace will flow throughout the world.
     Let the people sing "Hosanna" to the One who us enfolds.

2.   "Glory be" through saints and angels who proclaim the Savior's birth.
     Christ is born to every age through men and women of the earth.
     Once in flesh, Christ came among us. Still God calls in human form,
     sending prophets to awake us, makes each day a Christmas morn.

3.   "Glory be to God in heaven for the Christ who came to earth."
     Reconciled and sin forgiven, we can claim new life, rebirth.
     So we sing with all the angels, sing and praise your holy name:
     "Alleluia, come Lord Jesus! Come and lead us home again!"

"Celestial Secrets: The Sequel to 'Glory Be!'"

The Advent Angels Come Clean

Following the success of the first Advent play, I was asked to: "Follow that!" So this second play is deliberately a sequel to the first and expands upon it. The format is similar but with a shared leadership through a larger number of MCs. We also created a modern version of the medieval "Shepherd's Play" to add more humor. Telling the three stories from "Glory Be!" as a simultaneous event enabled us to see the pattern in the Divine plan, while sharing some "Celestial Secrets" proved to be both entertaining and informative.

Once again, costuming was left up to the cast, with the rule being "all white with gold or silver accessories." The keyboardist arrived as Mozart, complete with wig. "Historical characters," including shepherds, wore something approaching historical costumes.

Also used from the first year was the tradition of giving a white feather on a silver or golden thread in the worship aid and the blessing at the end of the service.

See the "Music Suggestions and Sources" section for further details.

CAST
MCs   1–8
ANGELS   (A 1–4)
SHEPHERDS   (SH 1–4)
Historical Characters:
     ABRAHAM and SARAH
     ZECHARIAH and ELIZABETH
     JOSEPH and MARY

Opening Song: [*Suggestion: "O Come, O Come Emmanuel," vv 1–4*]

MC1   Welcome once again to an evening with the Gabriel Division of the Holy Angels Flying Corps.

MC2   For those of you who were here last year, we thank you for returning.

MC1   And for those of you who were not, hold on to your seats!

MC2   We really are very happy to be able to find time in our busy annunciation schedules to come back to St. (*name of church*) and join you for this evening. We angels enjoyed ourselves so much last year, and since you were so willing to invite us back, we thought we would tell you some celestial secrets, stories that, until today, only angels knew about.

MC1   Some of you are looking surprised that annunciations are still going on. Well, you'll find out tonight that we Gabriel Angels are as busy as ever. So, without more ado, please welcome, with their theme song from last year, The Gabriels!

All other MCs and ANGELS enter through the church, singing and greeting the assembly. They end at the front, possibly on risers, with a tableau.

"One" from A Chorus Line. [*Replace all the gender pronouns with "we."*] *At end, all but MC3 and MC4 sit.*

MC3   Thank you, thank you. Some of you look a little surprised that angels behave rather like a Broadway chorus. But you shouldn't be, not when you think of our job.

MC4   We have to spend all of eternity announcing important things, so it's vital that people notice! Otherwise it would be a waste of time.

MC3   That's right, the perfect balance of production and content, although, of course, the details are *never* left to chance. You'll find that when you get to heaven.

MC4   For example, and don't tell anyone else this because it's a secret, the celestial music is organized by a team, presently consisting of Mozart, Duke Ellington, and Janis Joplin.

MC3   Our annunciation scripts are all written by William Shakespeare, Lucille Ball, and Walt Whitman, inspired, of course, by the active involvement of the Holy Spirit.

MC4   Our choreography is all by Busby Berkeley, Martha Graham, and Dame Margot Fontayne …

MC3   … and Liberace has a new career in interior design. (*Possibly indicate a "Liberace" touch near the musicians, maybe gold lamé or a candelabra on the piano.*)

MC4   You may have noticed that there are people on that list from many different places, religions, and ways of life.

ALL   Surprise, surprise!

MC4   Actually it shouldn't be a surprise. It really just explains why we feel so much at home visiting St. (*name of church*). To be sure, it's like a little bit of heaven on earth! (*MC1 and MC2 come forward.*)

MC1   But to return to our story of the annunciations we have made, probably the biggest secret we can tell you tonight is that the first annunciation is still going on!

MC2   That's right. The first time God decided to bring something to birth, it was quite an event. In Hollywood, I think they would call it a "Big Bang."

MC1   Yes, the creation of the world, well, actually of the whole system of universes, was our first job. And the nice thing is, it's still going on.

MC2   New angels always start on this job. To begin with, they announce the opening of flowers or the falling of leaves.

MC1   They graduate to announcing the beginning of each new day and the lighting of stars.

MC2   And occasionally, if you are near angels when they are doing these jobs, if you listen carefully, you may hear them singing this song.

All ANGELS sing "Something More."

At the end of song, all ANGELS and MCs join assembly for their hymn.

Community Song [*Suggestion: "For The Beauty Of The Earth"*]

MC5   All annunciations since then have really been a playing out of the natural consequences of that first Big One!

MC6   Charles Darwin was on the right track; he just wasn't thinking on a big enough scale.

MC5   He knows better now!

MC6   However, there was one thing that he did not know, which has been a closely guarded secret since the beginning.

MC5 (*shocked*)   Are you going to tell them?

MC6   Why not?

MC5   Do you think they're ready for it?

MC6   No. But I've never let that stop me before.

MC6, with optional Angelic chorus, sings "The Man In The Moon" from Mame.

MC2   As we were saying, all annunciations since the beginning of the world are really a consequence of that first one. God so loved the world that was created that, as time passed, as each new phase developed, God found new ways to communicate that love.

MC1   Eventually, as one of your prayers to God says, "when the times had ripened and the earth grown full in abundance, you created in your image man and woman, the crown of all creation."

MC2   One of the ways God found to communicate love to creation and to you, the people, was to send you prophets.

MC1   And of course we were the ones who told you to get ready for them.

MC2   There are three annunciations we remember well.

MC1   And they are all linked very closely, even though they happened in different places and times.

MC2   Three different women—ordinary, yet extraordinary women—chosen to be partners with God in the message of love.

MC1   Oh yes, their menfolk had something to do with it too. (*They enter as their names are called.*)

MC2   The women were Sarah, …

MC1   Her husband was Abraham.

MC2   Elizabeth …

MC1   Her husband was Zechariah.

MC2   and Mary.

MC1   Her hus— (*corrects self*) her *fiancé* was Joseph.

MC2   God always wants to make things as real and practical as possible, which is why we are always announcing things being born—or being reborn. (*ANGELS 1, 2, and 3 enter and take positions.*)

MC1   In this way, God's love is always tangible, is always able to be held and caressed and kissed, just like a new-born baby.

A1   And the angel said to Abraham

A2   And the angel said to Zechariah

A3   And the angel said to Joseph

A1   Your wife

A2   Your wife

A3   Your betrothed

A1   Shall conceive with you

A2   Shall conceive with you

A3   Shall be over-shadowed by the Holy Spirit.

SARAH   And Sarah laughed and said, "How can this be? I am too old."

ELIZABETH   And Elizabeth opened her eyes wide and said, "You heard *what* in the Temple?"

MARY   And Mary was deeply disturbed and said, "How can this be, for I am a virgin?"

A1   And the angel said …

A2   … nothing is impossible to God …

A3   … and in due time each conceived and bore a son.

A1   And they were named Isaac …

A2   … John …

A3   … and Jesus.

A1   And each was beloved in the eyes of the Lord.

A2   And each was tiny in his mother's arms.

A3   And each grew to greatness in the service of God.

The six historical characters sing "The Gift You Are" by John Denver.

Community Song [Suggestions: "People Look East" or "Lo, How A Rose E'er Blooming"]

MC1   As you can imagine, we angels are kept pretty busy. Not only do we have to cover all your births and deaths (or *re-births* as we like to call them), we announce every action that is a moment of God's love coming to earth.

MC2   We are what you might call "Incarnational Specialists."

MC1   Which is pretty good for beings that don't, officially, have a body.

MC2   Actually, we borrowed these from some of your parishioners so that you could see and recognize us tonight.

MC1   We have a rigorous holistic exercise routine, which sometimes spills over into creations of our own. These prayerful routines have to combine beauty and skill with spiritual growth and wholeness.

MC2   Normally these routines are secrets, but would you like to see our latest active meditation?

General activity to lead everyone to positions, instructions to musicians, etc., maybe beginning with the sounding of a bell, or chanting "Om", then into cassette of ...

Dance: "Macarena" (only twice) This dance is, of course, very dated now. You might either substitute another one or make something up.

MC1   You probably need to know one of the secret angel rules after that. Rule number 43 states that all angels must take their work seriously, take their responsibilities seriously, but never, ever, take themselves seriously.

MC2   One group of people who never took themselves seriously was a group we all enjoyed seeing at one of the annunciations. They were the shepherds.

MC1   The reason they didn't take themselves seriously was because they were pretty much on the bottom rung of the social ladder. They weren't even allowed to go into the main part of the Temple because they were considered ritually unclean, just because they worked on the Sabbath, looking after their flocks.

MC2   They were looked down on by almost everyone. Sheperding was certainly not a profession anyone would choose and was not exactly the romantic image you have today of hearty men and lovable lambs.

MC1   Of all the people God could have sent us to, when the orders came through that it was to be *the shepherds* who were to hear the first news of the birth of Jesus, well, you could have knocked most of us down with a feather.

MC2   Actually, they took rather more persuading than your Gospel writers suggest. Getting them to leave their sheep was not an easy task.

ANGELS, except ANGEL 4, all sit. SHEPHERDS enter.

SH1 *(arriving)*   Evening, all.

ALL SHEPHERDS   Evening.

SH2   Cold night again.

SH3   Why can't sheep have their lambs in the summer, when it's warmer?

SH4   My wife says carrying a child is hard enough work without the summer heat. Maybe the sheep know best.

SH2   It's okay for the boss; he just stays inside with his fire.

A4   Er, excuse me ...

SH1 *(ignoring ANGEL)*   Yeah. We're the ones who have to stay out in the cold all night.

SH4   Well, my wife says we should be thankful to have a job at all these days.

SH3   Even if everyone despises us.

SH2   Maybe we'll get a better job next year, like in the big house of something.

A4   I said, "Excuse me" ...

SH4   (*ignoring ANGEL*)   Or maybe one of us will become rich, like King David, the shepherd who was made king.

SH1   In your dreams, Simon, in your dreams.

SH4   Well, my wife says—

ALL SHEPHERDS   *Oh* be quiet! / Shut up about ... / Your wife always has something to say ...

A4   You asked for it! (*Turning to the CAST and conducting them*)

ALL ANGELS and organ   "Alleluia." (*All stand. Sing one word from the opening or closing of Handle's* Messiah.)

ALL SHEPHERDS   What? / Who? / Yikes!

A4   Thank you! "Fear not," said the angel, for a mighty dread had seized the shepherds, "I bring you tidings of great joy."

ALL SHEPHERDS   What's he talking about? / Pardon? / Who *is* this? / What's going on?

A4   If you would all be quiet for a moment, I'll *tell* you! You are all considered by God to be just the sort of people that need some good news. So, I've come to tell you that, for a short time only, you can go to Bethlehem and see the savior of the world.

stunned silence

A4   Er, hello? Anyone hear me?

SH3   Would you mind repeating that?

A4   I said that today is born for you a savior, that is the Christ. You will find him wrapped in swaddling bands and laying in a manger. Like his ancestor, King David, who was a shepherd like you, this child, whose name is Jesus, is to lead his people to greatness.

SH1   You mean, like, beat up the Romans?

A4   Well, not exactly.

SH2   You mean, like, get us a better job?

A4   Closer!

SH3   How about somewhere warm to sleep?

A4   Well, the stable is much cozier than this barren hillside.

SH4   But what about the sheep? My wife says—

A4   (*interrupting*)   Not to worry, I and my friends will stay here to mind the sheep while you go and visit the one who will become the new shepherd of Israel and indeed of all those who wish to follow the One God.

SH1   I don't like it. It could be a trick to steal the flock.

SH2   We're only shepherds; no one ever invites us to things like that.

SH3   Nothing good ever happens to us.

SH4   Yeah, we'll never be anything else but simple shepherds.

ANGEL 4, joined by all the ANGELS, sings "He Who Knows The Way." Toward end of song, SHEPHERDS believe and exit with ANGEL 4.

Community Song [*Suggestion: "What Child Is This?"*]

MC1   Well, we've covered really more than just the Advent story by telling you that one. But then, I suppose the secret we mentioned at the beginning makes it okay. Our annunciations are, as they say today, "ongoing."

MC2   And Advent never really ends because the Christ is still waiting to be born again in you and in people like you. Advent will go on until Gabriel calls all of us to help in the final annunciation, not of the Christ-*child*, but of the Eternal Christ who will come to welcome us home, one final time.

MC1   Just imagine, everything will be free. Money will be just metal as art, and everyone who in this life has suffered loss, deprivation, loneliness, or pain will find the cure—forever!

MC2   That's right. God's promise is that salvation is free. All you have to do is realize you can't do it for yourselves and, with the humility of the shepherds, ask for what you need.

MC1   To tell you a secret … we even have a song about it.

All, possibly with solos, sing "That Great Come And Get It Day."

MC2   Well, there you have it. The Gabriel Division is going to be busy right up to the last day.

MC1   And we're always looking for new recruits, so when you get up there, give us a call.

MC2   In the meantime, we want to have you help us now and be commissioned as Angels of the Season of Hope, ready to announce the ongoing birth of salvation in the days ahead.

MC1   So we invite you to find the symbol of Angel Power that has been placed in your program that we might pray the Great Angel Commissioning Prayer of long ago.

MC2   So, heavenly angels, are you ready?

ALL ANGELS   Yes.

MC1   And earthly angels, are you ready?

ASSEMBLY   Yes!

MC2   So let's stand and let's go, and the answer is Amen.

MC1   Angels of Earth and Angels of Heaven,
        do you believe that the God of All
        is in love with the universe?
        If so, please answer Amen.

ALL   Amen.

MC2   Angels of Earth and Angels of Heaven,
        do you believe that the Christ will return
        to bring life and to save?
        If so, please answer Amen.

ALL   Amen.

MC1   Angels of Earth and Angels of Heaven,
        do you believe you are called to bring forth the Christ
        in your life and your love?
        If so, please answer Amen.

ALL   Amen.

MC2   In the name of God the Most High …
        In the name of the Source of all Life …
        In the name of the Spirit of Truth, …

ALL ANGELS   Amen, Alleluia, Amen.

MC1   Be commissioned as Angels of Good News and Hope …
        to bring comfort and joy
        to a world needing both …

ALL ANGELS   Amen, Alleluia, Amen.

MC2   Be brightness and light.

MC1   Be friend to the stranger.

MC2   Be a Gabriel to all who need one.

MC1   And let the people say:

ALL   Amen, Alleluia, Amen.

Community Song [*Suggestion:* "Glory Be" (*Tune:* ODE TO JOY, words at end of previous play, "Glory Be!")]

"Paradise Lost And Found"

A New Look at the Creation Salvation Story

This play was written in response to the question, "Why did Jesus have to be born?" When we accept the Genesis creation story as mythology rather than fact, the question continues, "If there was no real first Adam, why did we need a second?" While I believe creation myths are very important to any society, we, as Christians, do not know how to listen to those of the Jews. They have their ancient and wonderful stories, and we need ours, understandable in both the history and present of our lived experience. The aim of this play and service is to open the idea of "what if" we retold our creation myth in the light of the Good News and especially in light of the story known as The Prodigal Son.

The second theological point that was formative in the writing of this play was a discussion about the values of light and dark in Advent. While there is a clear, traditional understanding of what is meant by "darkness" in this context, the reality is that too often a comparison between light and dark is used offensively toward people of color. As a second matter for consideration, modern psychology also points to the benefits of entering into the darkness, or our "shadow side." It seemed, therefore, appropriate not to talk about the distinction between light and dark but about the true light and the false. That, I believe, is the bigger issue and the more truthful interpretation of our story and spiritual journey.

With these two points in mind, the part of God was written for three characters, played ideally by a woman (GOD 1), a man (GOD 2) and a child/youth (GOD 3). The casting of these parts should represent the widest possible diversity of the community in age, ethnicity, and personal style. A very important note for those playing these parts is that God is *never* vindictive or negative in what is said. Even when tried or questioned or facing rebellion, God responds with care and love and humor, wanting only the best for creation. Sadness turns to yearning as God encounters the entry of evil into creation, but God is also clear about how to "turn it around." God is always God.

In creating this service, the costuming was once again fun, with the three God characters being dressed in a similar traditional style (long, white, elegant gowns with gold over-garments) but not identical. Adam and Eve wore regular simple clothes in neutral colors with a 1960s, ethnic look, while Lucifer, starting like all the other angels in a long white alb with a little silver or gold decoration, shifted into a white tail suit with blood-red satin shirt or roll neck.

During the song "Beautiful, Beautiful World," cast members enter dressed in the style of the 1930s Zeigfeld Girls, complete with hats or headdresses and representing the first five days of creation. Again, the casting of this group can represent the full age and ethnicity of the community. They may even be non-singing cast members, if that enables more people to be involved. I recommend two or three people per "day." The idea is for each costume to represent just one of the following elements: sky, stars, sun and moon, water, land and mountains, vegetation, flowers and trees, birds, fish, animals. The fullness of creation should be just that—full and color-rich, extravagant and abundant.

The staging involved a "choir area" in the back as the place where the cast could sit most of the time to be present but not intruding on the action. In the main action space, we used small risers to give the option for levels, especially necessary for the group scenes and the "Zeigfeld" song.

CAST
GOD 1–3
ANGELS 1–7 (A1–A7)
LUCIFER
YOUNG ADAM
YOUNG EVE
The ZEIGFELD CREATION GIRLS
OLD ADAM
OLD EVE
MARY and JOSEPH

Scene 1

Blackout, synthesized "space" music

ANGELS, including LUCIFER, enter and are grouped in "choir area."

VOICE OFF   In the beginning there was nothing: no earth and no universe. Nothing had been created. Only God and the angels existed, living in Paradise. And everything was perfect.

Lights up in "heaven" part of stage. Synthesizer music transitions into first song.

All ANGELS sing "The Music That Makes Me Dance" from Funny Girl. *This song could begin as a chant, with the angels in traditional prayerful poses. They could then "break out" on the word "dance." I suggest returning to a prayerful pose for the ending.*

GOD 1, 2, and 3 enter.

GOD 1   All right, all right, all right. Listen up, angels, do I have news for you.
GOD 2   Today we start creating the world.
GOD 3   That's right, today is the first day of creation.
A1   Creation? What's that?
A2   Yes, who needs creation? We've got Paradise.
LUCIFER   Everything's perfect. Why change it?
GOD 2   Because, quite simply, I want to. I am God, after all.
GOD 3   And as God, I can do anything I want.
GOD 1   And as God, I have decided I want to share Paradise with a whole world of created plants and animals and beings.
LUCIFER   Share Paradise! But why?
GOD 3   Lucifer, what's wrong? Are you jealous?
LUCIFER   Of course not, I just don't see why you would want to spoil a good thing like Paradise by putting mere created plants, animals, and beings in it.
GOD 2   I know they won't be pure spirits like us, but that doesn't mean they'll spoil it. I think they'll complete it.
A3   What exactly are you going to do?
A4   And how, exactly, are you going to do it?
A5   And what, exactly, do you want us to do?

GOD 3   Well, I've decided to begin by sharing a most precious gift—light. Besides, that way we'll all be able to see what we're doing. So Lucifer, since your name means "light bringer," you get to help start this great event off by bringing light to the darkness of chaos.

LUCIFER   I'm not sure I want to.

GOD 1   Well, with you or without you, there is going to be light, so why not go along with the program for the moment, and we'll see if I can convince you to like the idea in time.

drum roll or similar

ANGELS   And God said:

GOD 2   Let there be light (*other lights slowly up*)

LUCIFER   And there was light. (*Drum roll/music climaxes and ends.*)

GOD 2   There, that was not so hard, was it?

LUCIFER   No, I suppose not. But what exactly is the relationship going to be between these created things and us?

A3   That's right. We're pure spirit. These created things and beings will be messy. They'll even change! They'll do things like be born and get old and die. We're not used to that; we're always the same.

GOD 3   Yes, I've noticed that! Tell me, Lucifer, have you ever created anything yourself?

LUCIFER   Of course not, you know that all we angels do is what you command us to do.

GOD 1   That's true, I suppose. Well, I'm going to give you a special gift. I want you all to help me create this world of mine, so that you will experience and understand what it feels like to be a creator.

GOD 2   And that way you will know what the relationship will be between us and what is created. Don't you think it would be fun to experience what it's like to be friends with something or someone that is unpredictable?

LUCIFER   No!

GOD 3   Don't you feel that Paradise is all very nice, but it would be much more enjoyable if eternity was not so consistently the same?

GOD 1   Like, not being so self-focused all the time, even.

LUCIFER   I'm not sure I want to be part of this "creation," as you call it. It sounds unnatural to me.

GOD 2   Well, with you or without you, this creation will come about. Why don't you think about it a little more? It really could be fun.

GOD 3   In fact, why don't you all think about it? To be honest, I'm getting a little sleepy with all this work and conversation. How long have we taken so far just to create light?

A1   In earth time? 4 million, 300 thousand and 20 years.

GOD 1   Well, let's call it "A Day," shall we?

A2   And so that is how evening came and morning came: the first Day.

GOD exits.

Advent Carol

Scene 2

A4   So, what do ya think? Do we want to get involved in this "creation" thing?

A5   Sounds fun to me.

A6   I'd have to see the rules first. I mean, I don't want to mess up.

A7   I'm the same. Anything I create would have to be perfect.

A4   I think the idea is that we're the perfect ones, and God is getting a little bored with us, so he actually wants something a little more, how shall I say, improvisational.

A6   Does improvisation have rules?

A5   Oh yes. Rule 1 is "Start doing something." Rule 2 is "If someone copies you, change what you're doing." And rule 3 is "Once everyone knows the rules, change one of them."

A7   I used to think you were a nice angel, but I'm having my doubts.

A4   Doubts are allowed.

A6   No they're not! We're angels. We're meant to be perfect. That means we don't doubt.

A4   Really?

A5   Don't worry; we're only teasing. God will let us know the rules in good time. All I know is that if it's God's idea, it's going to be a good one, and I want to get involved.

A7   I'm not sure Lucifer does. After that conversation yesterday, I think there might be fireworks today.

A6   Lucifer's problem is that he wants to be in charge. He was really put out he wasn't made an archangel like Gabriel, Michael, Rafael, and Ariel.

A7   I didn't think we could have those sort of feelings. Isn't jealousy and envy rather un-angelic?

A4   I think it's similar to the way some angels need to know the rules, while others like the idea of improvisation. God created us all perfect in our own way but different from each other. Lucifer, as the light-carrier, needed the quality of being rather out there and noticeable, otherwise, what's the point of him doing the "light" thing? With his gifts, he could never have been, for example, the Angel of Quiet or Peace.

A5   Unfortunately he seems to forget that we're meant to work as a team with God, not as some Pavarotti or Streisand.

A4, 6, 7   Who?

A5   Oh, I forgot, you're not the Angel of History like me. Don't let it worry you; you'll all find out in due course.

A1   Places everyone, here comes God.

GOD enters.

CAST sings "Holy, Holy, Holy."

GOD 3   Thank you very much, as ever.

GOD 2   Yes, you sing that very well.

GOD 1   They should; they've been singing it for more than 400 million years. Don't you think it's time for a new theme tune?

GOD 3   But it's a tradition.

GOD 1   Sometimes traditions have to change.

GOD 2 Even this one? Well, I suppose we could ask them to try something new.

A2   Actually, we had been practicing a new one, just in case you ever wanted to change. Would you like to hear it?

GOD 2   Well yes, okay.

All ANGELS sing "One." [All pronouns changed to "you."]

GOD 3   I like it!

GOD 2   Excellent!

GOD 1   It looks like tradition can change after all. Anyway, back to the task of creating the world. Is everyone ready?

ALL (*except LUCIFER*)   Yes!

GOD 2   Lucifer?

LUCIFER   I still don't see why you want to do this. I know it is going to be a big mistake because it will mess up everything here in Paradise.

GOD 3   Paradise will change, I grant you, but change is not a bad thing. In fact, when it causes us to think and challenges our un-questioned traditions, it is generally a good thing.

LUCIFER   Well, I'm not sure I can go along with this whole thing. It's against my better judgment—and you wouldn't want to overrule my judgment, would you?

GOD 1   Of course not. You are excused, Lucifer, from joining in the rest of this wonderful experience of creating. But remember this: With you or without you, it will happen.

LUCIFER   Are you going to take away my title?

GOD 2   No. God does not take back gifts that have been given. You are still the bearer of the light.

LUCIFER   Thank you.

GOD 2   You're welcome.

GOD 3 (*cough*)   I think it is time to get on, don't you?

GOD 1   Yes. What shall we create today?

GOD 3   Well, what can we see down there? Angel of Vision, report, please?

A4 (*going forward and taking a long look*)   Eh … water.

GOD 3   Water.

A4   That's all I can see, water. Everywhere. Water above, water below, water to the left of us, water to the right of us. If I weren't an angel, I'd be drowning.

GOD 1   Now isn't that interesting. What's not Paradise is water. Who'd have ever known?

LUCIFER   It's amazing what you can see when you have light around.

GOD 3   I thought you didn't want to play?

LUCIFER   I don't. I'm just commenting. So, is this creation of yours going to be just in water?

GOD 2   No, but it is going to start there. All life will start in water. It will be indispensable from existence. Everything will come to life; everything will be made new from water.

A5 (*to assembly*)   Just in case you haven't noticed the significance of that statement, I'd like to point out, as the Angel of History, that both Darwin and John the Baptizer were right. Thank you.

GOD 1   Just as life will be in a cycle, so will the water that keeps it being reborn. Let's take a line through the middle of the water and lift it and turn it into clouds. There! Now there can be a sky and an earth, and there is the water on the earth and there is the water above the earth.

A6   Excuse me, but how will the water in the clouds get back down to the earth and the water on the earth get up into the clouds?

GOD 1   I'm not sure. But why don't I make you Angel of the Weather, and when you've worked it out, you can let me know.

A6   Oh, thank you—I think!

A1   And God looked at the vault that separated the water above the earth from the water on the earth, and God saw that it was good, and God said:

GOD 3   That's cool!

A3   And so evening came, and morning came the second day.

Music up: "Beautiful, Beautiful World"

A2   Okay, by now you are probably getting the hang of this. The next three days, which took approximately fourteen billion years to complete, saw first the creation of the land, separating it from the sea.

A1 (*interrupting*)   Day 3 done.

A2 (*continuing*)   Then the greening of the earth, everything from flowering plants and fruit-bearing trees to seed-laden bushes and grain-filled grasses …

A1   Day 4 done.

A3   And then the filling of the water above the earth with birds and below the earth with fishes, both of every sort, color, and size.

A2   Day 5 complete.

A1   And God looked around at all that had been made, and God saw that it was good, and God said:

GOD 1   I feel a song coming on.

GOD 1, 2, and 3 sing first verse of "Beautiful, Beautiful World." All, except LUCIFER, join in for the rest of the song. The ZEIGFELD CREATION GIRLS enter during song and take up places on risers, behind ANGELS and GOD.

Advent Carol [During this carol, GOD exits and then the ANGELS, except LUCIFER, return to their places for carol, then exit. LUCIFER looks at creation and then sits and muses about what has happened.]

Scene 3

Enter GOD 1,2,3.

LUCIFER   Well, are you finished creating? I have to say, it's not so bad after all.

GOD 1   Thank you, Luce, it's pretty good for a first time, even if I say so myself.

GOD 3   But no, it's not finished.

GOD 2   Even though I myself am in all of this, there is still something I want to create to bring together the best of heaven and the best of earth.

LUCIFER   Why do I have a sinking feeling?

GOD 1   One final gift ...

GOD 2   ... to bridge the world of creation ...

GOD 3   ... and the world of Spirit.

GOD 1   I am going to make something in my own image, male and female I will make them, and I will breathe my Spirit into them. And so they will be my children, and I will be their God.

GOD 3   I will call them each by name, and together we will walk in the world.

GOD 2   They will tend this garden of creation for me, showering it with love just as I shower them.

LUCIFER   And you will love them more than us.

GOD 2   I cannot love more, or less, than totally, and I love you totally.

LUCIFER   But they will be your children, and we are just your messengers.

GOD 3   Lucifer, God's love is freely given. You have as much as you can hold. Do not be jealous that I have enough to give as much to others.

LUCIFER   I am not jealous. But you are making a mistake. These creatures will never be as faithful to you as we are.

GOD 1   Lucifer, with you or without you, I *will* create in my own image.

LUCIFER   So be it. (*LUCIFER bows; GOD 1, 2, and 3 exit. The ZEIGFELD CREATION GIRLS exit, leaving Lucifer alone.*)

LUCIFER sings "Wherever He Ain't" from Mack and Mabel. *The male pronoun throughout should be interchanged with the female one and with the word "God." Suggest changing the opening dialogue to: "This ninny of a puppet was available the second that God called. And all she had to do was yell, 'Hey, Lucifer,' and this dumb, light bringer crawled. For seven lousy days ... "*

LUCIFER exits to rear of church, opposite the direction of "Heaven," where the ANGELES normally are. Music continues to cover the entrances for the following scene.

Scene 4

The ZEIGFELD CREATION GIRLS enter and take up positions as before. ADAM and EVE enter. ANGELS enter and move forward, one at a time, to inspect God's handiwork.

A4   They look like fun.

A5   I think they'll do.

A6   God is really amazing when it comes to creating.

A7   In the name of all the angels of Paradise, welcome.

EVE   Thank you.

ADAM   Yes, thank you.

A1   The change is amazing since God created this wonderful world and, now you. I mean God was always great, but there is a mellowness about the place now that wasn't here before.

A2   Even declaring that we are now in the Day of Rest—it's great to see how God is about all this and you. Imagine, now that you're here, God can rest! You need to know that you have brought everyone much joy.

EVE   You're embarrassing us.

A3   Well, get used to it sister, because you are very special; you make God smile and laugh in a way that we never could.

A4   And what makes God happy, makes us happy.

ADAM   It's very easy to make God happy when you live in Paradise. It's peaceful and everyone is so kind and encouraging.

A5   That's why it's called Paradise!

A6   But seriously, you do know about the trees in the center of the garden, don't you?

EVE   Of course, the Tree of Life and the Tree of the Knowledge of Good and Evil.

ADAM   And we know we are not to eat from them—and so we won't.

EVE   But I am curious to know *why* we cannot eat their fruit.

A7   The Consequences.

ADAM and EVE   Consequences?

A7   Yes, consequences. Everything has consequences. The consequence of eating apples or oranges is health. Eating grapes is fun too, but some foods are not so helpful. Too many prunes—and they will have their revenge!

A6   The consequence of eating from the trees in the center of the Garden is "responsibility."

EVE   But we have that already, we have to look after all the animals and be good stewards of the earth. We are responsible. (*ADAM and EVE begin to be affectionate with each other. This continues and embarrasses the ANGELS.*)

A5   True, but presently you are responsible *under* God. If you eat from the trees, you will be responsible *to* God. That is very different.

A4   Presently, if there is a problem, you just tell God and it gets fixed.

A3   If you eat from the trees, you would be telling God that you don't need that help anymore and that you can fix everything yourself.

ADAM   But why would anyone choose to do all that?

A2   If they had any sense, you're right; they wouldn't. But you have free will. You have the choice, the option, to be—

A1 (*interrupting, not able to stand the affection between ADAM and EVE*)   I think we've said quite enough, and I'm sure they get the picture. Besides, it's getting late and I think we should be getting along, if you know what I mean.

ALL ANGELS   "Yes?" / "Oh right," / "Of course," / "Look at the time," / "My, My."

Exit all ANGELS.

ADAM   What was all that about?

EVE   I think they're still getting used to being around humans. They get embarrassed very easily.

ADAM   I think they're going to have to get used to it, don't you?

ADAM and EVE sing "You Are Woman, I Am Man."

Advent Carol [During carol, ADAM and EVE exit, followed by the ZEIGFELD CREATION GIRLS.]

Scene 5

Enter GOD 1,2,3 along with ADAM and EVE. ADAM carries GOD 3 on his shoulder and sets him/her down, and then they play "tag" or something for a while.

GOD 1   There is nothing finer than to walk through this wonderful garden with you both.

GOD 2   I must say, you're looking after it very well. Any problems?

EVE   Thank you. No, no problems. The flowers are all blooming, the trees are full of fruit, and the animals, birds, and insects are behaving themselves. We had a small problem with the mosquitoes the first day, but once we talked to them, everything has been fine. They've developed quite a taste for bruised plums that are on the ground.

ADAM   Same with the snails. They would insist on eating the flowers before they bloomed, rather than wait until after. We had a pleasant chat about it, and now everything is fine.

GOD 3   I spoke with the angel in charge of weather about your watering schedule. Is everything running smoothly now?

EVE   Fine, thanks. Every third day we have a light shower for two hours from 2–4 AM. Works great!

GOD 3   Good, that's what I'm here for.

GOD 1   Anything else?

ADAM   I don't think so.

EVE   Not unless there is anything you can think of?

GOD 2   No. This is working exactly as planned. Thank you; you both make me very happy.

EVE   It's really us who should be thanking you. This place is wonderful.

GOD 3   Paradise!

ADAM   Yes, Paradise.

GOD 1   Well, time to move on.

GOD 2   Sweet dreams.

GOD 3   And may your dreams come true.

Exit God 1,2,3.

ADAM   You know I have this feeling I could really enjoy this Paradise for eternity. God is so easy to work with. Even though we're only part of the creation like everything else, we're so trusted.

EVE   I think I saw a twinkle in God's eye just then, as if we were being told something.

ADAM   Pardon?

Enter LUCIFER, in changed costume, opposite direction from heaven. S/he walks through space unseen by either ADAM or EVE until he speaks. He could even be up on the risers, looking down on them.

EVE   That last bit about dreams. What are yours?

ADAM   My dreams? I don't know. Er … well, I suppose I want to do this job well. I would like to be creative myself, I suppose, you know, add something to this wonderful place, leave my mark on it. You?

EVE   The same. Living in such a place makes me feel I could do so much. In fact, I think we may have already started creating something.

ADAM   What do you mean?

EVE   Oh you can't see it, yet.

ADAM   Why, where is it?

EVE (*aside*)   I have a funny feeling men are always going to be the same. (*back to ADAM*) You can't see it because at the moment it is—I don't know how this works—still growing. Inside me!

ADAM   Inside—oh wow! You mean like those rabbits we saw the other day?

EVE   And the young birds.

ADAM   We have created something!

EVE   Yes, and with the help of God, we will be as careful of this creation as we are with what God has made.

ADAM   Shouldn't we tell God the good news?

EVE   Call it a woman thing, but I think God already knows.

ADAM   I'm so grateful that I can share Paradise with you.

EVE   Good, 'cause I feel the same.

LUCIFER   Hello, how are you?

ADAM (*They see him for the first time.*)   Hello, fine, thanks. Er, I don't think we know you?

LUCIFER   No, we haven't met before. My name is Lucifer, the light bearer.

ADAM   I'm Adam.

EVE   And my name is Eve. How do you do?

LUCIFER   Fine, thank you, and I am delighted to hear your news.

EVE   Oh!

LUCIFER   Yes, I'm sorry. Angels do have a habit of overhearing things, especially good news.

ADAM   Do you think God knows too?

LUCIFER   Absolutely, that's why I'm here. God is overjoyed at your news, so I am here to help in any way that I can. I was, after all, the one who helped God on the first day of creation, so it is appropriate that I should be here to help you on the first days of yours.

EVE   What did you do for God?

LUCIFER   I help create the light. And my job is to lead people with light, to open their eyes to what is around them and what is inside them. Now that you are going to be parents, you'll have a lot of responsibility; you'll need to learn a lot of new things. I'm sure God will be very willing to help; all you'll have to do is call, and someone will be there.

EVE   It seems like an awful imposition. I feel we should be able to do it on our own.

ADAM   Yes, I don't want to keep troubling God with all my inadequacies.

LUCIFER   I know exactly what you mean and, in fact, there is a very simple solution.

ADAM and EVE   What?

LUCIFER   Come and eat from the trees at the center of the garden.

ADAM   But they are forbidden to us!

LUCIFER   True, they are called the forbidden fruit, but that is just God's way of keeping something special until the right time. You'll soon learn that trick as parents.

EVE   The right time?

LUCIFER   When it is needed, like now. You need to know how to bring your new child into the world, so you are going to need a lot of wisdom. Well, the tree can't give you that, but it can give you knowledge, and from knowledge you can grow into wisdom. I mean, God wouldn't have created it if it wasn't meant to be eaten, agreed?

ADAM   Yes, I suppose, but I'm still not happy about disobeying God.

LUCIFER   You wouldn't be really disobeying God, not if you understood how everything works, I mean, well (*music starts*), I suppose I shouldn't say this, but …

LUCIFER sings "The Apple Tree."

At end of song, LUCIFER leads ADAM and EVE off.

Advent Carol

Scene 5

ANGELS enter.

A1   What's happened?

A2   Haven't you heard, they ate from one of the trees.

A3   And that fruit sure worked fast!

A4   I heard they were tricked by Lucifer.

A5   Yes, he was there all right, even helped them reach the fruit by bending a branch down for them.

A3   No sooner had they taken a bite when their happy-go-lucky attitude left them.

A6   And they started noticing things, especially that they felt sad.

A1   What's going to happen next?

A2   Surely God will forgive them; I mean it was understood from the start that there would be problems, right?

A4   Yes! And the whole thing about not eating the fruit was for their benefit, not God's.

A5   It'll just mean a lot more work helping them make right choices. But that's not impossible in Paradise.

A7   The problem is that they're no longer in Paradise.

ANGELS (*all others*)   What?

A7   When they started noticing things and feeling sad, Lucifer told them that they must have been unworthy to eat the fruit, that they had eaten the fruit for their own benefit and not for the good of others, so God was going to be angry. He actually told them that their best chance was to get out of the garden before God caught them. He even offered to light their way to the quickest exit.

A4   And so they're gone?

A7   Yes, they've run off into the wilderness.

A6   I feel so sad.

A1   But God can bring them back?

A7   Only if they want to come back.

A3   Only if someone can find them first of all!

A1   What's going to happen next?

A7   They only ate from one of the trees; they only have knowledge. They didn't eat from the Tree of Life, so, as they are now outside Paradise, they will start knowing death. The only way they can come back into the garden is if someone takes them the fruit of the other tree, the Tree of Life. They need to eat of that tree before they can re-enter Paradise.

Enter GOD 1,2,3.

GOD 1   I notice the leaves on the trees are beginning to turn brown and die.

GOD 2   The birds have stopped singing.

GOD 3   And I am sad for the first time.

GOD 1   Lucifer, in spite of all his protestations, has, indeed, created something, something that I could never have created.

GOD 3   Absence, loss, the need for repentance.

GOD 2   Lucifer has created a false light by taking my gift and using it against me.

GOD 3   And yet I still love him.

A4   What can we do?

GOD 1   Angel of Vision and Angel of History, show us what has become of my children.

OLD ADAM and OLD EVE enter.

A5   Adam and Eve are now grandparents. Cain, the child they were expecting when they ran away, has brought them sorrow. He killed his younger brother, Abel, and then he, too, ran away. They had a third son, Seth, who is their joy. He has a son of his own and now Eve sings her grandchild a lullaby.

OLD EVE sings "Lost In The Stars."

A1   She looks so happy with her grandson.

A2   Both she and Adam have changed.

A3   They seem wiser but sadder.

A4   The Tree of Knowledge was a mixed blessing.

A5   They're finding out how many things they *don't* know!

A6   They're having to find out the rules of living in the world outside Paradise. That's not easy.

A7   How are you going to bring them back?

GOD 1   Someone has to take them the fruit of the Tree of Life. Without that, they cannot live in eternity.

A1   When Eve looks into the eyes of her grandchild, I think I can see a *glimmer* of eternity.

A2   It's almost as if Adam and she have not forgotten all they knew from here.

LUCIFER enters unseen.

A3   Maybe we could grow the tree for them and they could eat it by accident.

A4   Maybe not.

GOD 2   Eating the fruit of the Tree of Life will have to be a deliberate act, just like the one that caused them to leave the garden.

A5   But that was not their fault.

A6   Lucifer tricked them.

GOD 3   Then you and I will have to lead them to wisdom.

LUCIFER   You were right! This creation game is fun. These children of yours are really very amusing. Wisdom would spoil the game.

GOD 1   Why are you doing this?

LUCIFER   Doing what? I told you beginning this would only lead to problems. "Stick with the program," you said. "With you or without you," you said. What does it feel like to be God and make—a mistake?

GOD 2   I did not make a mistake. Love is never a mistake.

GOD 3   It will be your mistake if you think you can come between me and my creation. I have too much love.

LUCIFER   Have it your own way. You gave them their senses; I just work with what you made.

GOD 1   But I still had to teach them wisdom. Without it, their senses are incomplete. That is what I was doing in the garden before you led them away. Now they will know so much, but understand very little. They ate the fruit too soon.

LUCIFER   You should have thought of that before you gave them free will.

A7   Why are you dressed like that?

LUCIFER   Like it? It's the benefit of being the light bearer. I can bend the light to show anything I want. Light is a wonderful thing. It can be blinding and it can be dazzling. It's so easy to follow. These creatures of yours love it. They follow me anywhere. They are so hungry for light, especially since they left Paradise, they grasp at every little glimmer I send their way.

GOD 3   Enough. Your light is false. As much as I love you, I must ask you not to use my gift again.

LUCIFER   No biggie. There's enough light in the universe now to keep me going for thousands of years.

GOD 1   Thank you, Lucifer, you have just helped me solve the problem of how to lead my creation home.

LUCIFER   I did? How?

GOD 2   I will send a new light into the world, one which neither you nor anyone else will be able to put out. My true light will lead my children to eat of the Tree of Life.

GOD 3   I will lead them to a banquet, a huge celebration.

GOD 1   I will set out a table of all that is finest in Paradise and call them to eat with me.

LUCIFER   They'll never come.

GOD 2   We'll see.

LUCIFER   You can't create a new light; I won't allow it.

GOD 3   Too bad, Lucifer, the game is no longer yours to play. Your light is now ended. My light is coming into the world—and it will dance!

ANGELS (all)   Dance?!

GOD 3   Dance!

LUCIFER   Bah! We'll see! (exit)

Enter JOSEPH and MARY, they stand opposite OLD ADAM and OLD EVE.

A1   And God's word echoed across the universe and across time. God's word of light danced across the mountains and streams, across people and their lives and, in due time, it landed on a young couple in a town called Nazareth.

A2   And God sent the word of light into the life of Mary, and she conceived it in her womb, a light so pure that the angels rejoiced at the sight.

A3   A light so bright that stars burned brighter and called the wise to its side.

A4   And blessed was the fruit of the womb, for it was the seed of the Tree of Life.

A5   And all creation began to dance with joy …

A6   … because the Tree of Life had been planted in the world …

A7   … and it would give life to all who recognized it as the true light of God.

A1   And God said:

GOD 1   That's good!

Enter the ZEIGFELD CREATION GIRLS during introduction to song.

ALL sing "Stairway To Paradise" to OLD ADAM, OLD EVE, MARY, and JOSEPH, with solos and parts as appropriate.

"A Family Christmas Tradition" (or "Follow That Light!")

A Dance-Along Nativity

Many people celebrate the Christmas season by joining in a "sing-a-long Messiah" or going to see a production of *The Nutcracker*. This service and play came from an idea of our director of youth ministry (who has a reputation for trying to combine several good ideas into one event because that's how children and youth are) to do a "Dance-a-long Nutcracker Nativity."

After we had laughed a lot, we began to realize this would be a wonderful way to celebrate a truly intergenerational Advent or Christmas carol service, combining music, readings, storytelling, congregational participation, and even a strong message about the real meaning of the season. It would also be a contemporary look at the traditional "Advent Service of Lessons and Carols" celebrated in many cathedrals and larger churches throughout the world.

To add a seasonal touch, members of the congregation were invited to come dressed as either an angel, a star, a shepherd or stable animal—halos were provided with the service sheets for those who forgot and were willing to join in. Candles were also provided for each person for the final part of the service.

The Pastor led the service—as an angel.

CAST
CHILDREN 1–3 (C1–3, children speaking, others ad lib, non-speaking)
ADULTS 1–4 (A1–4)
ANGELS 1–3 (AN1–3)
SHEPHERDS 1–3 (S1–3; others, including children, could be non-speaking)
READER(s) for Scene 1 and Scene 4
STAR
STREET PERSON

Carol: "This Little Light of Mine"

Begins as solo with all the lights out. Choir and assembly join in after first time through. A single candle is processed in and used to light all the other candles in the space, ideally all around the church, but do not light the personal ones held by the assembly at this point. Once all the main candles are lit, the church lights are put on.

Opening prayer by Pastor

> Gracious God of our Lord Jesus Christ,
> in this Advent season we gather, once again,
> to tell the story of how much you love us.

We remember that you are a God who asks us
to make every day a Christmas for the world around us.
We remember that you want to be born in us today and every day.
Loving God, be here with us as we enter once more into the story;
inspire us to hear it in a new way,
like the children we are in our hearts, whatever our age.
We ask this through your great love for us shown in Jesus
and in the power of your Spirit,
you who is God for ever and ever,
Amen.

Carol: "Christ the Light Is Coming" [*Tune:* NOW THE GREEN BLADE RISETH]

Scene 1: "Children Ask the Darnedest Questions!"

Music from The Nutcracker *begins playing as the family (A1–3 and C1–3) enter and set up a table, some of the nativity scene, and the Christmas tree. They are decorating the tree and wrapping gifts. Once the music dims, the dialogue begins. Mary and Joseph are the only model characters put into the nativity set at this point. The others are added appropriately in the later scenes.*

C3   I'm glad it's Christmas again. Time for some more presents.
C2   Yeah, like ..... and ..... . (*Insert the names of the latest toy craze.*)
A1   Not a hope!
Cs'   Ahh (*general cries of pain*).
A2   Christmas is more than getting gifts.
C3   That's not what it looks like at the mall.
A1   Where did we go wrong?
C2   You didn't go wrong. You've produced wonderful twenty-first century young adults.
A3   With all the sensitivity of twenty-first century consumer monsters.
C3   We know Christmas isn't *just* about getting things, but it is the best bit, isn't it?
A1   I have to admit, getting presents—and giving presents—is fun.
A2   Be careful with those scissors and that tape, please.
C1   So why do we give presents?
A2 (*pause*)   No idea.
C3   Seriously, you don't know?
A1   It's something to do with the gifts of the shepherds and the magi. Right?
C3   Good try. That certainly has something to do with it.
A3   Is it something to do with St. Nicholas in Europe, giving gifts to all the poor children?
C3   Warmer.
A2   Okay, what's the answer, Oh Holy One?
C3   The answer is—(*interrupted*)
C1   ... because Jesus comes as a gift from God to save the world.
A1   I knew we sent you to Sunday (*or insert local school*) school for a reason.
C2   And we also know why we celebrate the birth of Jesus in the middle of December.
A2   Because that's when he was born?
C2   Wrong! Because December 24th is Midwinter's Day. That's when the Romans, and everyone else in the Mediterranean, started celebrating the feasts of their sun gods, near the winter solstice. When the earth was at its coldest and darkest, they worshiped the sun and asked it to return.
C3   So the Christians celebrated their feast of the Sun of God at the same time. And sort of for the same reasons. Don't you listen at all on Sundays?
C1   Right! Advent prepares for Christmas because it is about the end of the world.

C3   We celebrate the first coming of Jesus so that we can get ready for the second coming. Everyone knows that!

A3   Okay, so we know why we celebrate on *that* date, but I still have a question.

C2   Do I get the (*insert toy name*) if I can give you the answer?

A3   We'll see. My question is: Why did Jesus have to be born at all?

A1   (*pause*)   That's a hard one.

A2   No, it's not. It's obvious.

A1   I don't think so.

A2   It's obvious. Jesus was born to save the world. The Bible says so.

A1   But why? What was there to save? And how did he save it?

A2   That's .... He .... You have to remember that God's ways are not our ways. But I know the answer is right.

C2   It's easy. Because of Adam and Eve.

A2   That's right, because of Adam and Eve.

C3   But no one believes Adam and Eve were real people, like Santa— (*interrupted*)

As'   Shhh!

A3   I think the answer is that God loves stories. And the story about Adam and Eve and the story about Christmas are ways in which God teaches us about how to live life.

C1   I don't like the Adam and Eve story. God gets angry.

A2   God gets upset when people don't do the right thing.

C1   So do you, but you wouldn't throw us out the house if we were naughty. Not even if we were really bad. Would you?

A1   Of course not.

A3   Of course not. Maybe we need a new story about Adam and Eve. One that makes sense to our Christian ears rather than the Jewish ones for whom the original story was told.

C2   Do we get a prize for doing all this? (*They have been decorating the tree and wrapping presents.*)

A2   Sure, come on. (*All exit.*)

Music could cover the family leaving and even continue under the reading.

Reading: Leaving Eden

READER   God walked in the Garden of Eden and called to the woman and the man: "Eve, Adam, come and walk with me in the cool of the day." But neither appeared, just a voice from behind a bush which said: "We cannot come to you; we're naked!"

"So?" said God, because God knew they were naked. But then God sighed, "So!"

And the hurt in God's voice echoed around the Garden, and Adam and Eve felt their hearts grow cold. And Adam said: "I was tempted and I ate!" And Eve said: "I was tempted and I ate." And God said: "I am tempted ... " But God could not finish the sentence because tears were flowing like mountain streams after winter rains, torrents of tears, watering the earth and washing away God's anger.

And the serpent was caught in the tide and was swept away, all the time cursing the God who cried.

Meanwhile, Adam and Eve wanted to hide from God's tears, so they ran until they became lost in the wilderness, the farthest from God's dwelling place.

And when God knew they had gone into the wilderness, God lamented and cried: "Now do you see why I asked you not to eat from the Tree! I gave you a soul and breathed my spirit into you. I would have led you to know me with your heart. But you have chosen the way of knowledge and reason.

"You have chosen rather to know me with your mind. And so you will want to understand me, rather than to just be with me.

"And because you cannot understand me, you will feel accursed in your pain and your yearnings. Because you cannot understand, you will know what it is to suffer and sweat, and you will ask, 'Where is our God?'

"And when you cannot believe that I can understand your pain, you will know my loneliness instead.

"As for me," said God, "I will set a lamp on the Tree of Life, and I will send out my Son to find you and to show you the way home. I will stand at the highest point of my dwelling and watch so that whenever you wish to return I will see you and will come and meet you by the Tree."

Carol: "Come Thou Long Awaited Jesus"

Scene 2: The Lost Star

The STAR enters singing, possibly "City Lights" or another up-tempo number.

STAR   I love being a star! Well, who wouldn't? You see, I'm really a night person. I love being out there, brilliant against the deep, dark night sky, glowing with incandescent luminosity. Of course, I haven't always been a star; my beginnings were much more mundane. But that's all behind me and now, here I am—a star! And even if I say so myself, I'm fabulous at it.

It takes great skill to be a star, great determination and dedication.

But I stuck at it and then, one day, I got my big break, my own private big bang!

There are, of course, literally billions of us: all beautiful, all bright, all bejeweled in light.

However, I think of myself as being rather special because, and I share this in all humility, I was brought into being for a very special event.

Would you believe that I was born to be the star that signaled the birth of Jesus? Yes, I was. Moi. Little me. I was the star shooting across the sky, guiding angels, shepherds, wandering magi and even the occasional other star, showing the way to Bethlehem.

That's me there (*points to star on top of stable*).

Actually, I'll let you in on a little secret: I've decided to go into show business. I mean, I'd be a natural—a star!

I can see it now. I'll be the star of theaters and concert halls.

I'll be top of the bill at shows and galas. (*Intro begins.*) I'll bring a little glamour and style to the poor, hum-drum life of people, well, like you.

Song: "The Greatest Star"

STAR   Want to join me? Why don't all you wonderful stars come out here and shine a little? Come on. Everyone who has ever wanted to be a star, now's your chance!

Dance of The Stars [Music from The Nutcracker *on sound system, suggest "Waltz of the Flowers."]*

Carol: "Creator of the Starry Sky"

Scene 3: Shepherds and Angels

Enter CHILDREN 1–3.

C1   Come on, let's put the shepherds into the stable.
C2   Those dumb shepherds. I think we ought to put someone more interesting into it.

C3   Yeah, like Drew Carey or someone. No! I've got it: Darth Vader!

C2   Don't be stupid. Darth Vader's a baddy. He wouldn't come to worship the baby Jesus.

C1   He would as Anakin Skywalker, before he becomes bad.

C3   Yeah, and then the angels could know it was him and attack the stable.

Enter SHEPHERDS 1–3 and ANGELS 1–3, interrupting. General pandemonium.

S1   What do you think you're doing?

S2   You can't play around with us like that.

AN1   Those're my wings you're crushing; be careful.

S3   I am tired of people thinking that shepherds are stupid.

AN2   Okay everyone—quiet! Thank you.

AN3   What do you think you're doing, messing with us like that?

C2   I'm sorry, we just thought we would bring it up to date a bit, you know, more like something we could understand.

C3   Yeah, shepherds are not very big in ..... (*insert your city*) right now. (*Laugh.*)

C1   We don't know what shepherds do or why they were picked to hear about Jesus being born. Were you very important shepherds or something?

S2   All shepherds are important!

S1   Actually, that's not really true. Around the time when Jesus was born, shepherds were not thought of as important at all, or even as being nice people. They were very often really poor people, or even homeless.

C1   You mean like illegal aliens?

AN1   What's with the "alien" thing already?

S1   Maybe. I'm not sure what an alien is.

C3   An alien is a thing from outer space, and they eat human beings and have big, sticking-out eyes and suck your blood and—(*interrupted*)

AN2   Your friend needs to watch a lot less television.

AN1   Or stick with PBS.

S3   Shepherds were not popular people in those days. We had to work every day, especially during the lambing season, when we had to stay out on the hills all night. If we had taken the sheep into their folds, the poor little newborns might get stepped on.

C2   Yuck!

S1   So we stay on the hills, where there is room.

S3   Mind you, we have to stay on watch because of the wild animals. They might come and try and take the young lambs away.

C2   Double yuck!

C3   So why did you leave them like that— all alone on the hillside with no protection? Just 'cause some angel said there had been a miracle? They could have been joking—or have been aliens and tricking you.

AN3   We were not, *are not* aliens, okay?

C3   Okay!

C1   Was it *very* cold on the hillside in the winter?

Shepherds begin to nod, looking for sympathy.

AN2   I hate to tell you this, but it wasn't winter.

C1   What?

AN2   Sheep have their lambs in the spring, so the weather was not too cold.

C3   You mean you didn't need your winter wings on?

AN3   I'm getting close to turning this one into a spider or something. Somebody stop me!

C1   If you worked every day, when did you go to church?

S1   We didn't go to the synagogue, that's what we call our church. They wouldn't let us in.

C2   That's not very nice.

S1   No, not nice at all.

C3   So, like, you were outcasts. People were prejudiced against you, just because you did this job.

S2   We were lucky to have jobs.

C1   So why did the angels come to talk with you?

AN1   The angels were sent by God to tell the people the Good News.

AN2   And we decided that the people who needed to hear the Good News the most were the shepherds. After all, they were the most outcast of regular Jews at that time.

AN3   People who had been outcast from their own group.

C1   That was nice of God, wasn't it?

S3   Yes, it was. Very nice.

AN3   God is always nice.

C2   You mean like crying when Adam and Eve ran away?

AN1   Who told you about that?

C3   Er ... a friend.

AN2   Well, thank goodness that story got out, too.

AN1   God cries a lot, but we don't announce it too much because it would ruin the image. You know, all that stuff about being strong and all-powerful.

C3   Actually, this is the twenty-first century. It's okay to cry these days; even famous people do it.

C1   I think shepherds are nice people.

C2   What did you do when you got to the stable?

S1   We sang. We do that a lot while we are trying to stay awake.

C1   Will you sing for us now?

C3   Except can you make it in English and more modern?

Music starts.

AN1   I think it's time for another miracle!

SHEPHERDS sing verse 1 and a chorus of "The Swinging Shepherd Blues," followed by an instrumental verse, then another chorus, then going back to the opening interlude. During this interlude the following is said:

S3   Why don't all the other angels and shepherds in the church come and join us?

ANGELS and SHEPHERDS are invited to dance. Instrumentalists play through introductory section of the song and a verse, and then the dance ends with all the CAST singing a final chorus. At end, all exit.

Carol: "While Shepherds Watched Their Flocks"

Scene 4: The Outcast

Enter A1, A2, and STREET PERSON. The song "Free the People" begins under the reading. There is interaction between A1, A2, and the STREET PERSON. The STREET PERSON could be selling something, such as a newspaper.

READER   The Spirit of the Lord has been given to me,
for the Lord Yahweh has anointed me.
I have been sent to bring good news to the poor,
to bind up hearts that are broken;
I have been sent to proclaim liberty to those who are bound
and freedom to those who are in prison;

To proclaim a year of favor from Yahweh,
a time when God's ways will be done on earth.

STREET PERSON sings chorus from "Free the People."

A1 (*to audience*) I went out to do some shopping. It's hard not to see the parallels of the stable and the sidewalks. It's hard not to realize that I, that we, would never dream of going to a stable, or a barn, or to the projects (*insert name of a local run-down part of town*) to celebrate Christmas.
READER I have been sent to comfort those who mourn
and to take away their ashes,
and give them a garland instead.
To those who wear a shawl of grief,
I will give anointing with the oil of gladness.
And to those who are depressed, I will give praise and hope.

STREET PERSON sings verse 3 from "Free the People."

A2 It's not enough to understand the story. We have to make it come alive today. God still weeps for those who are alone, cast out. God still promises to hear the cry of the poor.
READER For I, Yahweh, love justice,
I hate robbery and all that is wrong.
I reward those who do right,
who live in right relationships,
and with them I make an everlasting covenant.

STREET PERSON sings chorus, verse 1, chorus from "Free the People."

Accompaniment continues and then ends during this reading.

READER I exalt for joy in Yahweh,
my soul rejoices in my God,
for I have been clothed in garments of salvation,
and wrapped in the cloak of integrity,
like a bridegroom wearing his wreath,
like a bride adorned in her jewels.
For as the earth makes fresh things grow,
as a garden makes seeds spring up,
so will Yahweh make both integrity and praise
spring up in the sight of the nations.

All exit during carol.

Carol: "The King Shall Come"

A3 enters during end of carol.

A3 The whole of creation was invited to the stable in the shape of the animals and birds. So let us bring them to our nativity scene too. (*The remaining statues, especially the animals, are placed in the nativity scene.*)

Dance of the Animals [Music from The Nutcracker, *suggest the dance of "The Sugar Plum Fairy."*]

Scene 5: Follow That Light!

Enter A1–3, C1–3.

A1   It's time to see if the lights work on the tree.
C1   Why do we put the lights on the tree?
A2   Well, why do you think we have a tree?
C3   Because it grows and is always green?
C2   Because it reminds us of the tree in the garden of Eden?
C1   Because it smells good!
A3   All those things—and because Jesus died on a cross made from a tree.
C3   So the lights are like the lamp God hung on the tree in the garden of Eden, to show Adam and Eve the way home.
A3   Light and candles have been used for thousands of years to show people the way home. That's why we leave the light on outside the door and why many people put lights in their windows at Christmas.
A2   And that's why we gather as a family at Christmas. That's why people travel, sometimes a long way, to get home for Christmas because it's a time to celebrate returning.
C2   But what about the people who have no home to go back to?
A1   That's a good question.
C1   Can they come here?
A2   We'll have to talk about that, but maybe. Maybe this year they can.

Carol: "Christ Be Our Light"

A1–3, C1–3 distribute light to assembly.

Intercessions: [*See example in the service outline for "Paradise Lost and Found."*]

Final Blessing and Commissioning

Carol: "This Little Light of Mine" or *"Carol at the Manger"* [*Tune:* BEACH SPRING]

An Advent Service Outline

Both "Glory Be!" and "Celestial Secrets" are self-contained, in that specific cast members preside as part of the script.

The following is the order of service that was used for the third play, "Paradise Lost and Found." It may also serve as a model for other services.

Gathering Song

PRESIDER   Welcome to the Advent Carol Service at St. (*Insert name of church.*) We are
delighted you have decided to join us in this celebration of the season of waiting for
the light.

Our salvation story has been told through many writers, beginning with the Book
of Genesis. Yet the story is ever new, just as we are called to be an ever-new creation
in the Lord. Tonight we are invited to listen with new ears as we wait for the coming
of the Light, the true light that reveals the unconditional love of God for all.

In preparation that we might hear the message of this season and the play, I invite
you to join me in silence for a moment, praying that we will have open hearts, open
eyes, and open ears for all that God wishes to speak to us tonight.

Silent reflection

Creator God of all that is good,
you who made the greatest stars and the smallest cells of life;
We wait in this Advent of your son for the Word that will save us and set us free.
Speak your word of life once more,
that we might celebrate this Christmas with the birth of a new Spirit within us,
that we might bring forth the glory of your name in a world that yearns for your light.
We make this prayer in the name of the light
whom you sent to be our Savior,
Jesus Christ, our Lord,
Amen.

*The play continues from the silence. After the play, the PRESIDER stands and invites the
assembly to join in the following prayers.*

Intercessions

PRESIDER   A hope-filled joy is the appropriate feeling for this season,
as we wait once more for the coming of the true light of God into the world.

Let us make our prayer tonight for ourselves and this world in which we live,
that we may all seek and follow the One who comes to save us.

Sung response

Loving God, the invitation to the banquet of life is your generous call to all humanity.
Yet many know only hunger, sadness of spirit, and exclusion from the tables of our
communal life because of their race, culture, gender, sexual orientation, health or
economic standing.
Open us to your inclusive love of all your creation, that we might share it with
everyone we know, the strangers we meet, and all those we are called to serve.

Sung response

The invitation to follow the true light that has come into the world means that we
have to be vulnerable to seeing the shadows that are cast by the choices of our lives.
In this season of Advent, may we be courageous in opening ourselves to the loving
glance of your light, that we might know the reconciling and healing power of your
love, and share it with everyone we know, the strangers we meet, and all those we are
called to serve.

Sung response

The invitation to be co-creators with you, gracious God, in the ongoing story of
salvation is the great gift of Christmas.
Remind us of our role in making you happy through bringing joy to your creation and
of the wonderful opportunity we have to dance our way to Paradise in the company of
all your angels and saints. Teach us the steps of our salvation, that we might share
them with everyone we know, the strangers we meet, and all those we are called to
serve.

Sung response

Closing Prayer

We are indeed called to walk, and even dance with each other
on the way of salvation, on the stairway to paradise.
May the God who has brought us to this place of joy and hope
continue to bless us in peace,
to shine the light of truth in our lives, and guide us to the banquet of love,
And may we be blessed in the name of the God
who is Creator, Savior, and Lover,
Father, Son, and Spirit,
now and for ever more.
Amen.

Our liturgy is ended,
Let us go forth, dancing the joy of Advent hope
out into a world that needs so much to hear it.

ALL   Thanks be to God.

Final song or joyous postlude [dancing optional]

Passion Plays

"No Greater Love"

The first of the Passion plays in this collection takes the familiar biblical text, from the tradition according to St. John, and, with a very few additions but particularly the songs, contextualizes it as a story of divine love caught in the path of very human politics. There are traditionally six basic scenes in the Passion play: Last Supper, Arrest in the Garden, Trial before Annas and Caiaphas (including the Denial of Peter), Trial before Pilate and condemnation, Walk to Golgotha, Death and Deposition. In these six scenes, a passionate story is played out about very human relationships against a powerful political reality that leads to murder. It is the power of these love relationships that provides the hope for enduring the force of destructive politics that brings death in its wake. To see the story anew, we need to focus not only on the central character of Jesus, but also on those who loved or loathed him.

The costuming for the play was entirely contemporary. Jesus could have come from any working or middle class family in almost any country in the world. Pilate is a tuxedo-wearing leader continually surrounded by minions and mistresses. Annas is a religious bureaucrat, more comfortable with the political and social scene than the streets. The biblical words attributed to these people should not be uttered with historical cobwebs hanging on them, but freshly, as if they were being spoken for the first time. They have edge, emotion, and economy.

The staging included only a large cross (12' high, cross beam of 8') with a set of risers so that the person playing Jesus could stand on the top riser and easily place his hands through ropes already on the crossbeam. As such, the whole event is played out under the shadow of the cross.

It is worth noting that this was not the first Passion play performed in the parish. The previous year we had narrated the full St. John Passion reading, divided into the scenes mentioned above, and mimed throughout using historical-style costuming. In between the scenes, traditional songs or instrumental pieces were played. It is good to ask the question whether your community is ready for a new look to this very heartfelt story. It might be worth getting everyone comfortable with drama, music, and mime in worship before appearing to "play" with the retelling of this particular story.

CAST
MARTHA
ANDREW
JESUS (S)
MAGDALEN (S)
PETER (S)
JOHN (S)
MARY (Mary the Mother of Jesus)
M. CLOPHAS (Mary, wife of Clophas) (S)

ANNAS
PILATE
DOORKEEPER
FIREKEEPER
SOLDIER 1
SOLDIER 2
DISCIPLES and FOLLOWERS of JESUS
Members of the SANHEDRIN
COURT (Members of PILATE'S court)
(S) denotes solo singing part.

Gathering Song: Suggest "Tree of Life"

During the gathering song, the Presider enters and waits in the middle of the space.

PRESIDER   I greet you in the name of God and in the sign of the cross, the Father, Son
and Holy Spirit. Amen.
May the Peace of Christ be with you.
ALL   And also with you.
PRESIDER   Once again we gather to remember the Passion and death of Jesus so that we
may more fully celebrate his resurrection.
Therefore, let us pray that we may be open to hear this familiar story anew tonight,
experiencing as if for the first time, the wonder of God's love for us.

Pause for silent reflection.

Let us pray.
Compassionate God,
you who call your people to walk
in the way of truth, the way
of Jesus your Son,
Be here with us as we remember
his Passion and the story which is never old,
the story of your redeeming love for all your
adopted daughters and sons.

Open our eyes and ears so that
we may hear and see the story anew,
that we may be moved to meet you again
in our neighbors who still experience the
journey to Golgotha.
We make this prayer through him you
sent to call us to holiness,
Jesus Christ our Lord.
Amen.

Suggested Assembly Hymn: "No Greater Love"

*During the final verse, the CAST enters and takes up positions as if at the Last Supper. It should
be a relaxed affair, passing around food and drink. They all continue quietly while MARTHA
and ANDREW come forward to talk to the assembly.*

Scene 1

MARTHA   We are here to tell you a story, a story about love. Not just the love of one person for another, but the love that flows out from people everywhere when they know they are loved even unto death.

ANDREW   And why are we telling this story? Well, as the evangelist John wrote at the beginning of his letter, we have something to share with you:

> Something which has existed since the beginning of time,
> that we have heard,
> that we have seen with our own eyes;
> that we have watched and touch with our hands:
> the Word, who is life—
> this is our subject.
> That life was made visible; we saw it and we are giving our witness,
> telling you of the eternal life that was with the Father and
> has been made visible to us.
> We are telling you this to make our joy—
> and your joy—complete."

MARTHA   So our story is one about love and joy. And yet it is more likely tears of sadness we shall shed before the evening is over.

Music fades up for "Thanks to You." Tableau becomes alive.

> Our story begins while Jesus is at dinner with his friends.
> It is the time of Passover and Jesus has chosen to celebrate one more time with his friends.

M. CLOPHAS and ANDREW return to the Supper.

MAGDALEN, JOHN, DISCIPLES and FOLLOWERS sing "Thanks to You."

Music continues and segues into introduction for "Eagles and Horses." The Supper scene is cleared away and all move forward.

M. CLOPHAS   After the Supper, Jesus left the house with his friends and disciples and crossed the Kedron Valley, a place well-known to them, for Jesus had often met his disciples there.

JESUS, (mimed) invites the disciples to stay nearby while he goes aside to pray. They fall asleep.

JESUS sings "Eagles and Horses."

At end of song, DISCIPLES are aroused by arrival of SOLDIERS.

M.CLOPHAS   Suddenly, Judas, one of us these past several months, arrived in the garden with a whole cohort of soldiers from the temple guard. They carried lanterns and torches and weapons.

JESUS   Who are you looking for?

SOLDIER 1   Jesus the Nazarene.

JESUS   I am he. (*pause*) I said, "I am he." If I'm the one you're looking for, let these others go free. (*PETER pushes forward to attack.*) Peter! No! Am I not to drink the cup that has been given me?

PETER   But …

JESUS   No. Just remember what I said and did.

Rumble begins on keyboard. JESUS arrested, DISCIPLES run. Segue to Scene 2(A).

Scene 2(A)

ANNAS and COURT enter. JESUS is brought forward. Music grows and dies.

ANNAS   Bring in the prisoner. Tell us about your teaching and why you gather disciples.

JESUS   I have spoken openly for all the world to hear; I have always taught in the synagogue and in the temple where all the Jews meet. I have said nothing in secret. But why ask me? Ask my hearers what I taught; they know what I said.

SOLDIER 1   Is that the way to answer the High Priest? (*He strikes JESUS.*)

JESUS   If there is something wrong in what I said, point it out; but if there is not, why do you slap me?

ANNAS   Enough!

They form a tableau. JOHN, PETER, DOORKEEPER, FIREKEEPER and SOLDIER 2, plus others, enter.

Scene 2 (B)

JOHN   Peter and I had followed close behind the soldiers. Because I knew some people who worked at the temple, I had been able to get into the high priests' palace. Peter was stopped at the door. (*To DOORKEEPER*) He's a friend of mine.

DOORKEEPER   Aren't you also a friend of that man they've just arrested?

PETER   No, I'm not.

JOHN   Wait over here by the fire. I'll go and see what I can find out. (*JOHN exits. PETER moves to fire.*)

FIREKEEPER   He's (*referring to JOHN*) a friend of that Jesus you know. Aren't you (*looking at PETER*) another of his disciples too?

PETER   No, I'm not.

SOLDIER 2   Yeah, didn't I see you in the garden with him?

PETER   I told you; I don't know that man!

They form tableau. JESUS turns and looks at PETER as music starts.

JESUS sings "Goodbye My Friend."

All exit.

Assembly Hymn

Scene 3

Enter ANNAS, JESUS, SOLDIERS, PILATE, and COURT.

ANNAS   Noble Pilate, we ask for judgment against this man.

PILATE   Well, what charges do you bring against him?

ANNAS   If we did not already know he was a criminal, we would not have brought him
　　　　to you.

PILATE   So take him yourselves and try him by your own law.

ANNAS   We are not allowed to put a man to death.

PILATE   What is the charge?

ANNAS   That he says he is King of the Jews.

PILATE moves to JESUS.

PILATE   Are you the King of the Jews?

JESUS   Do you ask because you are interested or is it what others have told you about me?

PILATE   Am I a Jew? It is the chief priests and your own people who have handed you over to
　　　　me! What have you done?

JESUS   Mine is not a kingdom of this world. If it were, my friends would have fought
　　　　to prevent my surrendering. My kingdom is not of this kind.

PILATE   So you are a king then?

JESUS   It is you who say it. Yes, I am a king. I was born for this and I came into the world
　　　　for it: to bear witness to the truth. And all who are on the side of truth listen
　　　　to my voice.

PILATE   Truth! What is that?

PILATE moves to ANNAS.

PILATE   I don't see you have a case against him. And, as it is a custom here that I should
　　　　release one prisoner for you at Passover time, I suggest I release your King of the
　　　　Jews.

ANNAS   We would rather have Barabbas than this man!

PILATE   Very well (*to SOLDIER*), release Barabbas and take this King of the Jews away and
　　　　scourge him. (*To ANNAS*) Maybe that will satisfy you.

*All exit. As they do PETER, JOHN, and MAGDALEN enter and watch JESUS go off. They sing
this song as if to him.*

PETER, JOHN, and MAGDALEN sing "Unexpected Song."

*PETER, JOHN, and MAGDALEN exit. Actors from Scene 3 return. JESUS has been scourged
and has a crown of thorns on his head.*

Scene 4

PILATE   I am going to bring him out to you and let you see that I find no case against him.
　　　　(*JESUS is brought in, maybe through the church.*) Behold the man.

ANNAS   Crucify him!

PILATE   Take him yourself and crucify him! I can find no case against him.

ANNAS   We cannot put a man to death. Yet we have the law, and according to that law he
　　　　ought to die because he said he was the Son of God.

PILATE (*to JESUS*)   You heard what they said. What is your answer this time? (*silence*) Are
　　　　you refusing to speak to me? You know I have power to release you, and I have power
　　　　to crucify you?

JESUS   You would have no power over me if it had not been given you from above. That is
　　　　why the one who handed me over to you has the greater guilt.

ANNAS   If you set this man free, you are no friend of Caesar's. Anyone who makes himself
　　　　king is defying Caesar!

PILATE   Here is your king!

ANNAS   Take him away! Take him away and crucify him!
PILATE   Do you want me to crucify your king?
ANNAS   We have no king but Caesar!
PILATE   That's right. And don't you forget it.

All exit except JESUS and SOLDIERS, who all move and wait at the side during hymn.

Assembly Hymn

Scene 5

At end of hymn, enter the women, JOHN, and other crowd members. JESUS and SOLDIERS walk towards the cross, meeting his mother and the other women on the way. JESUS is placed on the cross by the end of the song.

Women sing "The Angel Gabriel."

Enter PILATE and ANNAS.

PILATE   Hang the customary sign above his cross stating his crime. Let it be written in Hebrew, Latin, and Greek so that all may understand: Here hangs the King of the Jews.
ANNAS   You should write rather that this man *said* he was King of the Jews.
PILATE   What I have written, I have written!

They exit.

MARTHA   Near the cross of Jesus stood his mother and his mother's sister, Mary the wife of Clophas, and Mary of Magdala. There also stood his disciple John. They had always been especially close. In a final gift of caring, Jesus spoke to him and his mother.
JESUS   Woman, this is your son. Son, this is your mother.
    I am thirsty.
    It is accomplished.

JESUS dies on the cross.

MAGDALEN, JOHN, MARY, and M. CLOPHAS sing "Shattered."

ANDREW   It was Passover preparation day, and to prevent the body remaining on the cross during the Sabbath—because that Sabbath was a day of special solemnity—the chief priests asked Pilate to have the legs broken and the bodies taken away. So the soldiers came and broke the legs of those who were crucified with him.
M. CLOPHAS   But when they came to Jesus, they found he was already dead. And so instead of breaking his legs, one of the solders pierced his side with a lance. And immediately there flowed out blood and water, like a woman giving birth.

Some begin to take JESUS down from the cross and carry him out through to the back of the church.

MARTHA   After this, Joseph of Arimathea, who was a member of the Council but a secret disciple of Jesus, asked Pilate to let him remove the body. Pilate gave permission so he came with Nicodemus and others. They took the body of Jesus and wrapped it with spices in linen cloths, following the Jewish burial custom.

ANDREW   At the place where he had been crucified there was a garden, and in this garden a new tomb in which no one had yet been buried. Since it was the Jewish Day of Preparation and the tomb was near at hand, they laid Jesus there.

Assembly Hymn

According to local custom, there could now follow a period of silence or a veneration of the cross. The CAST should model what to do for the assembly.

CAST and choir sing, as an anthem, "The Flower That Shattered the Stone."

Final Blessing and Dismissal

"God of the Outcasts"

We are surrounded by Passion stories every day, just as we are surrounded by stories of great courage, joy, or despair. The power of Jesus' passion and death is both its universal nature and its specific reality. We continue to tell the story because of who he is and because of who we are.

In this play, it is suggested that only Jesus (and maybe not even he) is in historical costume. Everyone else should be dressed in contemporary clothes or just in black, and each cast member should be given a single item appropriate to his or her character. If the proposed cast is too large for the parish's resources, speaking parts can be doubled up and songs can be sung as solos rather than group pieces (or vice versa if you have a good group sound but not a good soloist). The cross may be real or mimed.

Use is made of mime in several places in the script, and of having two things happening together, to give a parallel effect. Directors should be free to deal with this as best fits the local situation.

CAST
NARRATOR 1 and 2
JESUS (S)
MARIA (S)
FRANCES
HOMELESS MAN
GIRL 1 and 2
WOMAN 1 and 2
MAN 1 and 2
BOY 1 and 2
CONVICT
GRANDMOTHER
SOLDIERS
PETE
PRIEST
Non-speaking prostitutes, alcoholics, victims of domestic violence, street people, and others with unknown problems.
(S) denotes solo singing part.

Order of Service and Play

Opening Song: Suggest "Tree of Life" or "My Song Is Love Unknown"

Introduction and Opening Prayer

First Reading (optional, from the season)

Psalm Response (optional, from the season)

The NARRATORS enter.

NARRATOR 1   The story of the Passion and Death of our Lord and Savior, Jesus the Christ, is a unique and yet common one. Many, before and since, have died more painful deaths. Many have died at the hands of violence for much less reason. So why do we tell this story every year at this time? Because it gives us hope. It gives us hope that in our experience of death we will also find faith in an experience of resurrection. The story of the cross is still being played out in the lives of people and communities throughout the world. It is through their eyes we will tell the story tonight.

NARRATOR 2   It was the time of the Jewish feast of the Passover and Jesus (*JESUS and rest of CAST enter, as if talking; they cross to center, JESUS stays, all others continue and exit.*), knowing that the end was getting close, wanted to share it one last time with his friends. And so he sent some of them off to prepare a place for them to eat.

JESUS sings "Papa Can You Hear Me?"

Toward the end of the song the CAST returns and take up positions in a tableau as if trees or rocks in the garden of Gethsemane.

NARRATOR 1   After they had shared the meal and sung the psalms, Jesus led them out to a place on the Mount of Olives. A garden called Gethsemane was there. It was a place the disciples knew well.

NARRATOR 2   "Gethsemane" actually means "oil-press." Most of us, at one time in our lives, have a Gethsemane experience, when the fiber of our lives is pressed out and we feel we are left dry and useless. The story of Jesus in the garden is the story of everyone who has suffered. Gethsemane was the place that Jesus met the pain of the world.

As each character speaks, s/he moves out from the tableau, speaks and then takes another pose, pleading to JESUS.

MARIA   I am the mother of three teenage children. When we moved to this neighborhood, it was a good place to bring up a child. But now, it is not safe. I worry.

HOMELESS MAN   I used to have a job and benefits. I was a good worker, and I tried hard. But I was "let go," got depressed, couldn't get a new job, and ended up on the streets. I used to have friends, or at least I thought I had some.

GIRL 1   I think I might be pregnant.

WOMAN 1   I'm a drug addict.

MAN 1   I'm an alcoholic.

BOY 1   I want to kill myself because I know I'm gay and I can't stand the prejudice and the fear of what will happen if people find out.

WOMAN 2   I have AIDS.

MAN 2   I have cancer.

CONVICT   I am a convict, yeah. But I'm not just a prisoner *in* the system, I'm a prisoner *of* the system.

GIRL 2   My father has Alzheimer's disease, and it tears me apart to see him like that.

BOY 2   I fear that by the time my generation comes to govern this planet, the greed of the older generations will have killed it for us.

GRANDMOTHER   I fear that I will be forgotten and left to wait out my days alone with just my memories.

NARRATOR 1   And Jesus went apart and prayed.

CAST (excluding JESUS), in the garden, sing "Out Here On My Own" divided between solos, groups, and all.

NARRATOR 2   Suddenly the palace guard and the soldiers (*They enter.*) arrived in the garden to arrest Jesus.

JESUS   Who are you looking for?

SOLDIER   Jesus of Nazareth.

JESUS   I am he. (*pause*) I said I am he. If I am the one you are looking for, let these others go free.

Music: "Dies Ire" from Verdi Requiem (or similar). Suggest using recording. Use as much as necessary and then fade out.

During this piece, the CAST try and fight off the SOLDIERS, unsuccessfully. They are scattered and JESUS is escorted away.

NARRATOR 2   So Jesus was arrested and taken to a nighttime meeting of the Council, where the Chief Priest and the elders, using false witnesses and motivated by their own fear, condemned him to death.

FRANCES and MARIA enter from different sides. MARIA is wearing an apron, carrying a teatowel. FRANCES rushes to her.

FRANCES   Maria, where are you?

MARIA   Here, in the kitchen. Why? What's the matter?

FRANCES   It's Nilo, they've arrested him.

MARIA   What? My son! What do they want with him? What could they think he has done?

FRANCES   Maria, you know they do not need to think anything. He is an honest person who tells the truth. Unfortunately, he tells it on the street corners and to their faces, so he is a threat. But—(*interrupted*)

MARIA   They will execute him, won't they? Like Paulo and the rest. No trial, no defense, no hope.

FRANCES   There is always hope. But you must be careful.

MARIA   No, I must be a mother. Where are Las Madres meeting tonight?

FRANCES   Outside the town hall, but it will be dangerous. The soldiers have guns, and it will not help Nilo's case.

MARIA   Nilo will not die alone, nor will his death be without some gain. Don't worry, the pain of childbirth gives us mothers a strength stronger than any soldier's steel.

MARIA and FRANCES freeze in a tableau on one side of the space. PETE and MAN 2 enter from opposite sides.

PETE   What'd the doctor say, Dad?

MAN 2   Er … Not good, I'm afraid.

PETE   What does that mean? Do you have to have some more tests? Do you have to take different pills, what?

MAN 2   I have cancer.

PETE   But you … I mean … Are they sure? I mean, it's operable, right? They can do something about it, yeah?

MAN 2   No. I have about three months, six if I'm lucky. (*break down*)

PETE   It's okay; I'm here. I'll be here, day and night. We can fight this together.

MAN 2   When I lost your mother, I thought I wanted to die. But now …

PETE   Dad, listen to me. You've heard the doctor's verdict, now hear mine. Who has the power, you or the disease? *You* choose how to spend the rest of your life, however short or long it may be. You've always been in control; don't stop now!

PETE and MAN 2 freeze in tableau opposite MARIA and FRANCES.

NARRATOR 1   People are condemned to death every day. Maybe it's a medical cause, and they don't have any insurance. Maybe they live in the Third World, and clean water is reserved for others. Maybe they are children who die from simple childhood problems in a state or country that we do not care to support with development money or even salt tablets.

Rest of cast from the garden scene enter and take up positions facing the assembly.

NARRATOR 2   Thousands and thousands of people are condemned to death every day because of the choices other people make. We should not be surprised that the same happened to Jesus. After all, he chose to be poor and outside the power structure. Why should it be any different for him than for the rest of God's anawim, God's little ones?

NARRATOR 1   And they asked Peter, "Do you know this man?" (*indicate the CAST*) And Peter denied Jesus, saying he had never seen him before. And then the cock crowed, and Peter realized what he had done and went away and wept bitterly.

NARRATOR 2   They gave Jesus a cross to carry and led him out.

JESUS, carrying cross, and SOLDIERS enter. They move through the church. JESUS falls at least once.

CAST sings "Shelter Of Your Arms" to JESUS, divided as appropriate into solos and ensemble.

If MARIA, FRANCES, and the person playing the PRIEST are part of this scene, they exit at end of song.

NARRATOR 2   On the way, he met the women of Jerusalem who wept for him. But he said to them:

JESUS   Why do you weep for me? Don't weep for me, weep rather for yourselves and Jerusalem.

GIRL 1 (*to assembly*)   Don't weep for me because I'm pregnant, just help me to find somewhere to live, to have my baby, to get a job and even some child care.

BOY 1   Don't weep for me because I'm gay; just stop telling your bigoted jokes and simply accept me for who I am.

WOMAN 1   Don't weep for me because I am a drug addict; just help me to get clean and then let me be useful again.

MAN 1   Don't weep for me because I am an alcoholic; just stop expecting me to be perfect at work and at home and do it alone to prove I'm a man.

WOMAN 2   Don't weep for me because I have AIDS; just treat me as you would any other human being, not like some social pariah.

JESUS   For the days will come when people will say happy are those who are barren, the wombs that have never borne, breasts that have never suckled.

GIRL 1   When this first happened to me …

BOY 1   … I wanted to die.

WOMAN 1   But then I realized …

MAN 1   … that death would come soon enough …

WOMAN 2   … and I need not wish it to come any quicker.
BOY 1 & GIRL 1   I will carry my cross …
MAN 1, WOMAN 1 & 2   … and I will help you carry yours … (*They pick up JESUS' cross.*)
GIRL 1   … because now I know that I'm not alone, and I never will be again.

JESUS and SOLDIERS and CAST carrying cross continue to place of execution. The following action is mimed.

NARRATOR 1   At the sixth hour, they reached the place called "The Skull." They stripped and crucified Jesus there, together with two others. They cast lots for his clothing, giving him vinegar to drink when he was thirsty. They ridiculed him and called to him: "He saved others, let him save himself." They left him there to die.
CONVICT   I know how he felt. Three strikes, three nails, what difference does it make? Either way, your life is over.
HOMELESS MAN   My three nails are no home, no job, and, after three months, no help. I'll die out on the street rather than on his cross or in his cell. But it's the same end.
CONVICT   Did I do wrong? Yes. Am I a repentant thief? Yes. Does anyone care? No.
HOMELESS MAN   What did he do wrong? Nothing. Like me, he was a victim of circumstances. The ones with safe jobs on the Council just decided to downsize the opposition, or, in my case, the support.
CONVICT   Jesus, son of David, have mercy on us!
JESUS   Truly, I tell you, today you will be with me in paradise.

Either one voice or several or all sings "Being At War With Each Other."

NARRATOR 2   It was the ninth hour and the sun was eclipsed. A darkness came over the whole land. The veil of the Temple was torn down the middle. And Jesus cried out in a loud voice and gave up his spirit.

CAST now form a procession as if going into church. Each picks up a red carnation, hidden in a basket. The PRIEST enters, robed for a funeral, followed by MARIA and FRANCES. They have their heads covered and are carrying carnations also, maybe rosaries, too.

PRIEST   Nilo Valerio is dead. Those who killed him desecrated his body. Those of us who believe and hope in the resurrection have something to hold onto while grieving over his untimely death. Many will say it is a pity someone so young and so dedicated should die so suddenly—and so violently. I feel I know Nilo quite well, even though we had not been in touch since his college days. Even then, he was already firm and clear-sighted about the path he would take. I'm sure he had his share of frustrations, difficulties, and doubts. The journey is long, and full of twists and turns. We travel with each other, changing ourselves as we try and change the world. More than once we will be tempted to give up, drop out, hold back. Like Nilo, we need the gift of final perseverance. For if we look at our life as some precious treasure we must hoard, the demands made by others of our life are like losses. And death is a final loss, a final failure to hold on to our life. But if we look at our life as a treasure we must share, every service we give to others is a fulfillment of our life's purpose. And death is the final giving, the total giving. And Jesus said: "Father, it is finished, into your hands I commend my spirit."*

MARIA sings verse 1 and chorus only of "Not a Day Goes By" by Stephen Sondheim from Merrily We Roll Along.

JESUS is taken down from the cross. As music continues the CAST, led by MARIA, lay their carnations on or near the cross. If possible, the assembly is invited to do the same.

Sacred silence

Intercessions

Final Prayer and Blessing

Song: Suggest "We Remember How You Loved Us"

*Source: "The Gift of Final Perseverance," *Celebrating One World*, CAFOD and St. Thomas More Centre (London: 1989).

"Come to My House"

The preface for this script is that for seven years I worked with CAFOD (The Catholic Fund for Overseas Development) in London, England. Throughout those years, I was honored to work with and meet women and men who were living with the poorest of the poor throughout the world. Their faith in the rights and dignity of the individual, every individual, was as powerful an expression of the Good News as can be imagined. Some of them, and their friends, eventually gave their lives simply by being who they were, where they were. Each denomination has its contemporary martyrs. This play is my homage to them.

Liturgically, this play was first performed the year that Lent began with the reading of Noah's Ark, the flood, and the rainbow, Genesis 9:8–17 (Lent 1, cycle B.) (See also "The Prologue" in this book.) This reading is a powerful one for me, ideally suited as a precursor to the Easter celebration. It also, however, reminds me that many in our world are still drowned under a continual deluge of greed, indifference, disempowerment, manipulation and, to put it bluntly, evil. "40 days" has been more than forty years for some, and they still search the sky for that tell-tale sign of the sun. Liturgy committees, play directors, and casts are invited to explore the metaphor of the rain that drowns and brings nightmares, and that other rain which brings new life and refreshment as a way to prepare for the production and the Holy Week in which it will be given. This exploration might take place through music selected, prayers written, and liturgical environmental design choices made throughout the Lenten season for the community.

The person representing Jesus had a small, separate acting area, backed by a cross, where he mimed the whole Passion story as it was told through the play, both the narration and the action. His moves were largely dictated by the moves of The Worker cast member and vice versa: When she was bound, he mimed the same; when he mimes breaking the bread, she does it; when she is placed in prison, he placed himself on the cross. In this way, both are seen to be telling each other's story.

The homeless people, who form the chorus, created a small encampment with cardboard boxes, brooms, large buckets, blankets, and the like. The Worker pushed a soup and coffee trolley. The Chief of Police and the Judge were both clearly, though differently "corrupt," and you are invited to use any contemporary allusions to bring home the point. Our Chief of Police always had a secretary that followed him everywhere. She had no words, but her face told many stories. Feel free to add attendants, mistresses and the like.

The "cell" looked like a sturdy jail door, with bars top to bottom and a mid-way support. It was made slightly on a curve, so that The Worker's body would lay easily against it. Handles were placed outside on the top and bottom, both sides, for carrying. Straps were placed on the inside top for The Worker's hands. After she is shot, the door is lowered by the guards from upright to horizontal, and the body carried out on it.

CAST
JESUS (mime)
NARRATOR 1–4
POOR PERSON 1–3
THE WORKER (S)
SAL (S)
POLICE 1–3
POLICE CHIEF
JUDGE
WOMAN 1–3
Various attendants, secretaries, officials, etc.
(S) denotes solo singing part.

Prologue

Enter NARRATOR 1–4.

NARRATOR 1   The Passion and Death of our Lord and Savior, Jesus the Christ. It was the time of the Passover festival. Jerusalem was full of visitors, and, to keep order, Roman soldiers. Relations had been strained of late between the largely self-governing Jewish community leaders and the Roman occupiers. Suggestions had been made, by those with connections to the Roman governor, that the zealots who periodically attacked and even killed loyal soldiers were doing so at the encouragement of the Temple. Reprisals would be swift and thorough if this was ever found to be true.

NARRATOR 2   Pontius Pilate had a bad reputation, even in Rome, for his supposedly "thorough" ways. The Emperor himself had complained of the enthusiasm with which the governor had, on occasions, dealt out punishment without regard for the process of Roman law.

　　Palestine was hardly a high-profile appointment and many said the area got what it deserved. So the Jewish leadership and the Roman ruler held an uneasy peace. A peace that was more fragile at festival time.

NARRATOR 3   No state governor or even city mayor likes a disturbance to mar a big event. It reflects poorly on their leadership.

　　And the bigger the event, the more "thorough" the clean-up job that must be done.

　　It makes little difference whether it is a first-century Passover or twenty-first century international meeting; the effect is the same. The place must look good for the visitors. It becomes the time to round up likely protesters, clean the streets of panhandlers and the homeless, and generally put a fresh coat of paint on everything.

　　In Berlin in the early 1930s, the building of Hitler's Olympic stadium required the moving of several hundred poor families from homes that had to be demolished to make way for the grand edifice.

NARRATOR 4   More recently in Sao Paulo, Brazil, thousands of impoverished day workers and domestics, dwellers of the infamous ramshackle slums, saw their homes bulldozed to make the place look clean for the world media and the participants of a Miss Universe Pageant.

　　And in order to prepare for important, international visitors to Manila from the World Bank during the Marcos regime, hundreds of people were removed with an efficiency that would make Pontius Pilate seem tame.

　　The Passion and Death of our Lord and Savior, Jesus the Christ, is also, you see, the passion and death of many less famous sons and daughters.

　　Yet their mothers too have wept, their friends have buried them, and their captors have also divided the spoils.

NARRATOR 1   And the Lord God said to Noah: "I shall place my rainbow in the sky, and it shall be a sign of the covenant I shall make with you and your descendants forever. Never again will I send rain to wipe you from the face of the earth."

NARRATOR 4   And Noah replied: "No, God, we can do that for ourselves."

Blackout; sound: thunderstorm. As it subsides, lights up.

Scene 1

Chorus of homeless people sing "Come To My House."

During song they enter and build the encampment. The WORKER also enters and begins to distribute coffee, soup, and food.

NARRATOR 1   On the first day of unleavened bread, when the Passover lamb was sacrificed, the disciples said to Jesus: "Where do you want us to go and make the preparations for you to eat the Passover?" So he said to them: "Go into the city and you will meet a man carrying a pitcher of water. Follow him."

General noise. POOR 1 enters, carrying pitcher, goes to group around fire.

POOR 1   Gawd, I swear this water gets heavier every day.

POOR 2   Just be grateful they haven't turned it off.

WORKER   They can't do that yet; we have a court hearing scheduled for next Friday. 'Til then we're okay.

POOR 3   When you're quite finished with "The Ten O'clock News," some of us would like some soup, please.

WORKER   Coming right up.

POOR 3   Didn't mean to be rude.

WORKER   No problem. Besides, whenever I get grandiose ideas that I should be doing something more important than this, you help me remember the most important thing is that I'm the soup lady.

POOR 2   Well, you might be the soup lady, but you're all right too.

WORKER   Thanks.

POOR 3   Er … while you're here, d'ya have any of them pills for Sal? She's been bad lately, what with the weather an' all.

WORKER   Depressed?

POOR 1   Worse than a eunuch in a harem!

WORKER   I'll see what I can do. Sal? Sal? It's me, Lizzie. What's wrong?

SAL   Nothing, hon. Nothing. I'm fine, I'll be fine. Don't worry about me, hon.

WORKER   Sal, have you eaten anything today?

SAL   Yes hon, I had a cup of coffee for breakfast.

WORKER   Here, have some of my bread. I baked it today. And here, put your hands around this nice cup of hot soup. There. Go on! Eat and drink.

SAL   It's like I'm drowning.

WORKER   What?

SAL   It's like I'm drowning. It's like this great wave of something that just comes at me and hits me and drowns me, and I can't do anything about it. Are they going to move us out from here? It's dry here and it's so cold and wet out, especially at this time of year. Are they going to let us stay? Can you stop 'em please?

WORKER   Sal, mind, you'll spill the soup! I don't know if they'll let us stay.

POOR 1   Us? Are you staying all of a sudden?

WORKER   I …

SAL   She can't stay. She has to go and make more bread and soup.

WORKER   Would it make a difference if I did stay?

POOR 1   No. You'd just be like one of us—and we need for you to be more than that. You being here gives us hope that we're not totally forgotten.

SAL   And you're a good cook!

WORKER   Thanks. Now why don't you get some sleep, and when I come back I'll bring you something that should take away the feeling of drowning.

SAL   Thanks, hon.

NARRATOR 2   After he had given them the bread to eat, the wine to drink, and had washed their feet, Jesus led his disciples out to the Mount of Olives. There, in the garden of Gethsemane, the disciples fell asleep as Jesus went apart and prayed.

Homeless sleep, more or less restfully.

The WORKER sings "God Help The Outcasts."

At end of song, rain sound effect starts.

SAL (*delirious, waking from a nightmare*)   I'm drownin', help me. I'm drownin', the river's coming, the water's rising, I can't swim. Help! I'm drownin'.

General moaning and complaining about the noise and then beginning to move because of the rain.

WORKER   It's okay; it's only the rain. I'm here. You're not drowning; I won't let you. Just hang on, Sal; just hang on.

Police arrive.

POLICE 1   Okay people, it's time to go.

More general confusion and noise.

POLICE 2   By order of the Council, this place has to be vacated by morning. So clear up your stuff and don't let us have any trouble.

POOR 1   Who do you think you are? We've got rights.

WORKER   These people have been here nearly a year. They're not doing anyone any harm, and there is a court injunction on the Council's action pending for next Friday. Besides, it's cold and wet out. Just because it's politically "not nice" to have a homeless problem, moving them on won't solve anything.

POLICE 1   We don't want any trouble, lady, we're only doing our job. Now pack up your stuff and move out, or we'll have to move you and cite you for obstructing a policeman in the execution of his duty.

WORKER   You can do what you like. These are my people, and I'm staying right here with them.

POLICE 2   No you're not.

Sound effects of thunderstorm.

The homeless disperse and the WORKER is taken prisoner.

Instrumental reprise, chorus "hum" "Come To My House." At end, rain effect ends.

Scene 2

NARRATOR 3   Jesus was arrested and taken to the High Priest's house, where an emergency meeting of the Council had been called, including the chief priests, scribes, and elders. The Sanhedrin was looking for evidence about Jesus on which they could pass the death penalty, but they could not find any.

    Eventually the High Priest stood up and put this question to Jesus.

POLICE CHIEF   Under the current emergency powers of the state, it is an act of treason to resist the forces of the law. Do you think you and your personal crusade are more important than the present safety and future prosperity of the nation?

WORKER   When the law is not based in truth but in manipulation, when the forces of law are more concerned with maintaining death squads rather than protecting life, then "yes," my personal crusade is more important than your law because mine is the one that is truly undertaken for our present moral safety and future prosperity.

POLICE CHIEF   A confession like that makes a trial unnecessary. You are a very committed woman; I admire that. But you are a novice in the ways of the real world. Your sort doesn't understand that everything must be compromised some time or another. God sends the sun and rain on good and bad alike. I just happen to prefer the sun all the time. Take her away.

As the WORKER is led around the space, various homeless enter and move out of their way. No one helps. A clock chimes.

NARRATOR 3   And so they led Jesus away to the governor's palace in order that Pilate might condemn him to death.

    Near the palace, Peter, a disciple of the Lord, stood warming himself by a fire. Three times he was asked, "Weren't you with him in the garden? Why you're a Galilean!" And three times he denied his friend saying: "I do not know the man!" At which time, the cock crowed for the second time. And Peter went away and wept bitterly.

Scene holds a tableau. SAL enters.

SAL sings "Daytime Nighttime Suffering."

At end, SAL exits.

Scene 3

JUDGE enters.

NARRATOR 4   Pilate questioned Jesus about his teaching and what the chief priests said of him, especially the claim that he was the King of Jews.

WORKER   I am not the leader of this gang, as you call them. They are just poor, homeless people, and I'm just the soup lady. I make bread for them to eat and soup to warm their malnourished bodies and spirits. That cannot be a crime, even in this godless place.

NARRATOR 4   Pilate asked Jesus many other questions, but Jesus would not reply.

JUDGE   Do you not realize that I have the power to save you and the power to condemn you?

WORKER   You would have no power over me if the ones in charge had not given it to you. And you will do what they say because you are frightened of standing up to them.

JUDGE   Why are you doing this?

WORKER   I don't know. To begin with, it seemed like a good idea, feeding the hungry and stuff. But over the years, I have come to know them as people. And now they are very important to me. They are like family to me. I can no more deny them than I can deny myself.

JUDGE   Even if it means death?

WORKER   I am not choosing death; I am choosing truth and fidelity. You are the ones choosing death.

A note is carried to the JUDGE.

NARRATOR 4   Seeing what was happening, the chief priests spoke to Pilate and said: "If you set this man free, you are no friend of Caesar's. Anyone who makes himself king is an enemy of Caesar's."

POLICE CHIEF   For the good of the state and national security, it is better that one or two people die than anarchy should reign. Don't you agree?

NARRATOR 4   And so Pilate handed Jesus over to be scourged and then crucified.

Chorus of homeless sing verses 1,3,4,5,6 of "My Song Is Love Unknown."

By the end of the song, the WOMEN are wearing simple white headscarves and all are carrying placards on which are faces of people who have "disappeared." Each one is over-written with "Dead," "Disappeared," or a similar word.

Scene 4

NARRATOR 3   As they took Jesus out to be crucified, the women mourned and wept for him.

POLICE 3   Who are you? What do you want?

WOMAN 1   We are the Mothers of the Disappeared. We come here every week to bear witness to our children and our friends who have been abducted and never seen again.

WOMAN 2   We come to ask for information. Why does our government feel threatened by poor peasants and social workers?

WOMAN 3   And why does the media not tell the truth about what is happening here?

POLICE 3   Mothers, go home. You won't make any difference. The government is only doing what is best for you. We have no idea where your family members might be. They will only be in danger if they are involved in subversive activities against the state.

WOMAN 2   We will not be silenced. We will walk in witness to the horror of what happens in the name of national security.

WOMAN 3   One day the murders will stop. One day the blood of the innocent will cry to heaven for peace.

POLICE 3   Go home now, before I have to arrest you for violating rules of the state of emergency.

WOMAN 1   Happy are the ones who have never suckled rather than have their children torn away from their breasts by monsters like you!

WOMAN 2   And may those who gave birth to you soon know the agony which we live each day.

POLICE 3   Get out of here! Go on, move!

Women are forced out.

Scene 5

The WORKER is brought to the "cell."

NARRATOR 2   When they came to the place called The Skull, they crucified Jesus there. They stripped him of his clothes and even cast lots for them.

POLICE 1   Here you are, your suite for the next little while.

WORKER   Where am I?

POLICE 1   Most of the residents call it The Ritz.

WORKER   Why can't you let me go?

POLICE 2   It's festival time. People are a little jumpy. The international media is in town, and your friends have been moved away so that everything looks nice and clean. We don't need you causing a problem for us right now.

WORKER   How long will I be kept here?

The WORKER is placed with her back to the "cell" door. Her hands are placed through straps, as if tied. She has her back to the assembly.

POLICE 1   You ask too many questions.

WORKER   How can I be dangerous? What have I done? Just feed a few people and bring them a little healing and love. Is that so awful?

POLICE 2   We said be quiet.

WORKER   I need to get a message to my mother and my husband. Will you do that for me?

POLICE 1   Lady, you don't seem to understand. As far as the rest of the world is concerned, you no longer exist. You've disappeared. That's right, just for feeding the poor and being their friend. That's all it took.

The chorus re-enter, with their placards and candles, as if at a vigil.

NARRATOR 2   At the foot of the cross stood Mary, the mother of Jesus, Mary of Magdala, Salome, and Mary, the mother of James, together with many of the women who had followed Jesus around Galilee.

At the ninth hour Jesus cried in a loud voice, "Eloi, Eloi, lama sabachthani?" which means: "My God, my God, why have you deserted me?"

WORKER   Oh my God, no! (*Gunshot. WORKER dies.*)

NARRATOR 2   And he yielded up his spirit.

The earth shook and the sky turned black. And the veil of the Temple was torn in two from top to bottom.

Thunderstorm sound effects.

Silence

SAL begins to sing "Someday," then all homeless join in.

JESUS mimes his resurrection and follows body of worker.

During the song, the WORKER's body is carried out on the cell door by the police. The homeless watch and sing. If there is to be a veneration of the cross, either use the one from the "JESUS" acting area or another one can be brought in afterward. Whichever is used, the veneration might begin by the CAST placing their placards and other items of costuming around the foot of it.

"Weaving Between Heaven and Earth"

Several factors were weaving their way through the community when this script was written. Not least among them was a concerted effort to involve more women in the liturgical telling of the Good News and, on another plane, the desire to find links between the various parts of the liturgical cycle.

Probably the most complex of the scripts in this collection, this Passion play was performed the Lent following the Advent we restaged "Paradise Lost and Found," with the character of Lucifer being recreated as a member of the Sanhedrin, under the name "Levi." The Advent question of "how do we find the true light?" was seen to run through the Gospels that year. Also current that year were questions about "what is the community?" We had explored this question through images of weaving and quilting in our liturgical environmental design, prayers, and even music from Advent onwards. The blending, indeed weaving, of all these questions and themes helped both create this script and, maybe more importantly, formed the context in which it was shared. However, having said all that, I believe it stands on its own merits and will work in many other situations.

All the characters wore historical-style costumes, and there was no set. Both the opening and closing crucifixions were focused over the heads of the assembly, at the back of the church.

CAST
The WOMAN
SARAH (wife of Peter)
MARTHA (sister of Lazarus)
MARY (sister of Lazarus)
BVM (Mary, the Mother of Jesus) (S)
MIRIAM (the woman at the well) (S)
LEVI (a Priest [also LUCIFER]) (S)
NATHAN (a Pharisee)
DAVID (a priest)
JOSEPH (of Arimathea, a priest)
PETER (the disciple)
JESUS
JOHN (the disciple)
JAMES (the disciple)
JUDAS (the disciple)
ANNA (a follower of Jesus)
NAOMI (a follower of Jesus)

RUTH (a follower of Jesus)
SOLDIER 1 and 2.
Other priests, soldiers, disciples, followers, and children.
(S) denotes solo singing part.

Scene 1

Blackout. Recorded music "Officium" is heard. The WOMAN enters and stands looking toward the back of the church, as if watching her son being crucified. Lights slowly come up. Others enter, as if passing by on market day. They stop to talk, look, move on. No one approaches the WOMAN. BVM, MARTHA, and SARAH enter.

SARAH   What's happening?
MARTHA   Another of those crucifixions.
BVM   That poor woman, what must she be feeling?

BVM goes towards the WOMAN.

MARTHA (*to BVM*)   It's better not to. What could you do? Besides, you don't want the soldiers to see you here.
BVM   Because?
MARTHA   Because they notice people—and your family is getting enough notice at the moment, what with Jesus and the way he came into town last week. These people see things and remember.
SARAH   Martha's right. Let's keep going. We can't do anything here.
BVM   What did he do?
SARAH (*reading inscription on cross*)   Seems like he was a zealot, probably caused a disturbance by trying to whip up the crowd to fight the Romans.
MARTHA   Don't they know it's pointless? No group of desert nomads is going to overthrow a Roman garrison.
SARAH   Can we go, please? That soldier is beginning to look at us and without Peter here, I feel scared.
MARTHA   Peter's a good man. But he also needs to be careful.
BVM   Martha, you're scaring her. Sarah, Peter is fine. Jesus and the rest of them are not looking to overthrow the Romans. They're in no danger. They'll be fine. They'll just stay in Jerusalem for the Passover and then we'll all be back to our villages, out of harm's way.
SARAH (*looking at WOMAN*)   She's so alone. No one wants to be seen with her.
BVM (*goes to WOMAN*)   Your son?
WOMAN   My son.
BVM   I'm sorry.
WOMAN   My son, who thought he could change the world! Now look at him. My husband is already dead. What can I do? My son. He was meant to take care of me. Now I will not even be allowed to bury him. My only son. No mother should have to endure this.
BVM   You're right; no one should.
MARTHA   Mary, we need to go. Please.
BVM   Where are you from?
WOMAN   Bethlehem, no one ever goes there.
BVM   Oh I know it well. My son was born there too.
   I will remember you over the coming Holy Days. May the story of our ancestors' passing over from Egypt to the Promised Land be a consolation for you, and may the bitter tears you cry today, like those of our ancestors in slavery, one day be turned to joy in the knowledge of the Messiah, of Yahweh.

WOMAN   My son said the Messiah would come if we called loud enough. My son said that if we cry to heaven for freedom from this slavery, we would be heard. Yahweh hears neither his shouts nor my crying. Yahweh is not sending a Messiah today, or any day soon.

The only Passover there will be for me this year is the Passover to death.

Everything I have in the world is hanging on that cross!

BVM   After the Holy Day, you must come to Nazareth. My son and I will make a place for you in our home.

MARTHA   Mary!

BVM   Just ask anyone for the carpenter's house. Please say you'll come.

WOMAN   I may. Thank you.

MARTHA   We have to go now; the others will be wondering where we are. Please, Mary.

BVM   I'll look for you after the Sabbath.

BVM, MARTHA, SARAH exit. Music rises, the WOMAN and crowd react as victim dies. All exit, the WOMAN last.

Scene 2

Enter JESUS, PETER, JAMES, JOHN, the rabbis/priests/scribes: DAVID, NATHAN, JOSEPH of Arimathea, LEVI and others.

LEVI   How dare you enter Jerusalem like some cheap traveling entertainer. Riding a donkey is no way for a teacher to behave.

NATHAN   And while we contest your right to call yourself a rabbi, for you have not been schooled as we have, it is unforgivable that you should make a mockery of our role and position. The people need us to be leaders in these times of trial and to behave appropriately.

PETER   I don't see what you're getting so anxious about; he's never called himself a rabbi.

JESUS   Peter, I don't think …

PETER   No, it's not right. These men think that because they're trained in the schools of the priests, they are our leaders. They're nothing but collaborators.

LEVI   Silence your disciple, Nazarene. Or we shall have to have him silenced for you.

PETER   Why you …

JESUS   Peter, this is not the time or place. Please.

DAVID   Why have you come to Jerusalem at Passover this year? The city is already full of visitors from all over. We don't need your sort, fouling the air with the Romans.

JESUS   I will do no fouling of the air with the Romans. The Romans are not part of the law of Moses. I have no need even to talk with them, although some of them seem to want to talk with me. My ministry is to the house of Israel.

NATHAN   Well, let me put your mind at rest and tell you that Israel is being well ministered to by us and those of the *official* priestly and rabbinic families.

LEVI   And we do not need your help—or hindrance.

JAMES   You have no interest but to load people up with laws and requirements. You even cheat them in the temple, exchanging their hard-earned money for your own coinage and selling only your animals for sacrifice. Not only do you do the killing for them, you make a killing off them.

DAVID   You sound like your Master this morning, ranting and raving about commerce in the temple's court of the gentiles. Quite a show it was, too, casting out the tradesmen and the exchange officials. Remind me to send you a bill for the tables you broke. Or maybe you'd like to repair them yourself, carpenter?

LEVI   If your ministry is to Israel, maybe you should have more respect for the holy place.

JESUS It is you who should have more respect, not only for the holy place, but for the holy people who are God's chosen. And you should have more respect for their faith, that seeks hope and finds only extra weights to carry.

DAVID I remember you saying that you came to fulfill the law, not demolish it. How things change!

JESUS The law of God is written in the hearts of faithful people, not on tablets of stone hung around their necks. Those hearts it is my duty to teach, those yokes it is my duty to break.

LEVI Once again you seem to think that just because the ignorant find you attractive because of your miracles, that you can claim the rights of a teacher of the law.

NATHAN You are not of the house of Levi, you are not a priest, so you cannot be an authentic teacher of the law!

JOSEPH My brother Levites seem to forget that our God has, occasionally, called forth prophets from other houses of Israel, although I have to agree with them that your behavior this morning was difficult to understand.

DAVID Joseph, you side with this man against us? Maybe in the country, in your Arimathea, it is permissible to challenge the law, but in Jerusalem it is not. Caiaphas himself ordered us to speak with this false teacher. Do you now distance yourself from our High Priest?

JOSEPH Caiaphas and I are old friends, and occasionally, yes, we have found ourselves on different sides of the debating table when it comes to interpreting the law. But we are still friends, and I do not advise you to speak on his behalf to me.

NATHAN Jesus of Nazareth, do you promise to leave Jerusalem within a day and to stop teaching falsely? Further, do you promise to stop your so-called miracles and return to your village and duties as a son and faithful follower of the law?

JESUS I am not staying in Jerusalem, but outside the walls. As to my teaching, I have never taught falsely. The miracles that you and the people see are not mine but are of God and my duties to both my family and the law are fulfilled wherever I am.

JOSEPH Answered like a true Pharisee! It's a shame your mother did not marry into the same family as her cousin Elizabeth. You would have made a wonderful priest.

PETER You mean like John the Baptizer?

JOSEPH Now there was a faithful follower of the law!

LEVI Let me put my brother's questions another way. In the name of Caiaphas, the High Priest and the whole Sanhedrin, and for the good of the whole people of Israel, you will leave Jerusalem immediately and you will stop teaching and leading the people astray. Do you understand?

JESUS I have always understood.

LEVI Good. You may go.

JESUS, PETER, JAMES, and JOHN exit. JOSEPH exits.

LEVI (*to one of the others or a servant*) See that they are followed and leave Jerusalem. If he returns to the city one more time, I want to know about it. I shall go to Caiaphas and Annas. Have the temple guard stand ready from now until after the Holy Days. This Passover will be quiet, one way or the other.

Scene 3

Song: A Psalm [See "Music Suggestions and Sources" section.]

BVM and the other women and children are sitting sewing, weaving etc., while they sing a psalm. JESUS arrives.

MARTHA If you're back, then the others must be also.

SARAH   Has Peter gone home? I want to talk with him.

JESUS   Yes, he's home by now. Although James and John are probably still with him.

SARAH   Goodbye, I'll see you tomorrow.

All the women begin to pack up their work and exit slowly.

BVM   Thank you Sarah, and don't be too hard on your husband. If you shout at anyone, it should be this one here (*indicates JESUS*).

SARAH   Don't worry—if anything ever happens to him, I'm holding your Jesus personally responsible, miracles or no miracles.

JESUS   Peter is a man, Sarah; he makes his own decisions.

SARAH   Maybe, but if he'd stayed a fisherman in Galilee, the worst that could have happened would have been a telling-off from the rabbi at synagogue. Remember, our villages are not overrun with Roman soldiers like this place.

MARTHA   Sarah, go home. Nothing's going to happen. Right, Mary?

BVM   I'm sure. Nothing is going to happen, is it? (*looking at JESUS*)

JESUS   I'm not going to do anything, I promise.

MARTHA and SARAH exit, the last to go.

BVM   Did you mean that?

JESUS   What?

BVM   That you're not going to do anything.

JESUS   Yes, as far as I know.

BVM   The women were talking about what happened at the temple this morning. What made you do that? Why, you're lucky you're not in the temple prison even now. Poor Sarah is terrified that if you get into trouble, Peter won't be able to help himself and he'll get imprisoned, or even worse. What's happening?

JESUS   What do you mean?

BVM   On the way back this afternoon, we passed one of those crucifixions. Promise me that you won't do anything stupid and end up like that poor young man. His mother was beside herself. Don't make me go through that. Please.

JESUS   I love you. And I would never do anything to hurt you. From the moment of my conception in your womb, you have nurtured and loved me. Never have I known a day when you did not fill my heart with compassion and prayer. Joseph and you made a home that flowed with laughter and joy. I'm sorry if anything I've ever done hurt you. Sometimes I know I've been so wrapped up in following what I truly believe is what God wants me to do I may have seemed ungrateful or distant. But …

BVM   Shhh. Don't be silly. I am so proud of you. No mother could want for a son that loved so well and spoke so beautifully about God and life and everything that makes us human. Look, I've made this for you for Passover. It's seamless, woven on a special loom. Mary and Martha showed me how.

JESUS   Thank you. Thank you, not just for this but for everything you're always giving me. Thank you for the life that's in me and the breath I breathe.

BVM   Oh, shhh now. (*Introduction to song begins.*) I'm your mother so listen to me …

BVM sings "I'd Give My Life For You."

Both exit at end of song.

Scene 4

Enter JUDAS and LEVI. There is a stand or table with a basket of apples on it.

JUDAS   You wanted to see me?

LEVI   Yes. You are a disciple of Jesus the Nazarene, correct?

JUDAS   Yes.

LEVI   By all accounts, if you'll pardon the pun, you are their treasurer, too.

JUDAS   We hold all things in common. People are very generous to Jesus for the work he does. We don't have much money, people usually just give us food or the offer of accommodation and the like, but what we have, yes, I look after.

LEVI   I would like to make a donation to your cause. From what I hear about him, I admire Jesus very much, although, of course, I've never met him.

JUDAS   You should; it might change how you think about life.

LEVI   How do you think about life, Judas? Tell me.

JUDAS   I think life is about being faithful to the law of God and about preparing for the full and complete restoration of the house of Israel as the place of salvation for the whole world.

LEVI   You answer well. You should have been a priest rather than a mere disciple.

JUDAS   I am happy with my lot.

LEVI   But tell me, how will this Jesus do what you talk about? From what I have heard, he has no army to overthrow the Romans. He is no David or even a Saul. Can Jesus the Nazarene be part of this great—and very worthy—dream you have?

JUDAS   I was a disciple of John the Baptizer. I knew him to be a man of God. He told us to follow Jesus. It is enough for me to know that I am faithful in these small ways. God will accomplish the rest.

LEVI   God can indeed do everything and we very little. But throughout history, God has chosen to work through the hands and lives of mortals in the story of revelation. Even our great father, Moses, recognized that fact. God chooses individuals to be the prophets and helpers of the revelation of God's immense love for us. And, Judas, I think that God has chosen you to be one of those prophets. Would you like some fruit? I picked them myself this morning from a tree in the temple grounds (*no response from JUDAS*). Well, here, take one for later. (*Gives him an apple.*)

JUDAS   Why would I be worthy to be chosen as a prophet of Yahweh?

LEVI   Oh, you're not. None of us is worthy. Even Moses was not worthy. All the prophets were very clear about that for themselves. I am not worthy to be a priest in the house of Yahweh. That is why we offer a sin offering before everything else. We are not worthy, you and I. But we try to be loyal instruments of God, vessels for the revelation of the divine.

JUDAS   I still don't see why you are talking to me like this.

LEVI   You are a zealot. Don't deny it. I don't mind. Many of your friends are trying to bring about the fall of the Roman garrison here in Jerusalem. I have to tell you Pilate is not worried that you will succeed, but he is tired of your trying. His patience is wearing thin and he takes it out on us. The religious freedom of Israel is in your hands.

JUDAS   How?

LEVI   I, too, believe that Jesus is the Christ.

JUDAS   You do? That's … that's amazing. But why are you not talking to him about this? Jesus was in the temple today and, from all accounts, your police almost arrested him and the others and threw them in prison.

LEVI   I know, I was able to stop the Sanhedrin doing that. But I won't be able to stop them for long. Which is why we must act, you and I.

JUDAS   You want me to help you?

LEVI   I cannot do it without you.

JUDAS   What must I do?

LEVI   If Jesus is the Messiah, the Christ, the Holy One of God, then he needs to come in power now, soon, before the Romans have a chance to destroy Jerusalem because of the terrorist attacks of your zealous friends. And God needs us to bring that revelation about.

JUDAS   Jesus is the Messiah, I know that in my heart. But he is not about to overthrow the Romans or anyone else for that matter. Yes, I am a zealot, so yes, I do believe that we must help God rid this holy soil of these murderous heathens.

LEVI   The Scripture tells us what to do. It is written: "God would not let you stumble, lest you strike your foot against a stone." If our savior was arrested and sentenced to death, then God would have to act and bring about the one thing that you and I and all of Israel longs for—the coming in glory of our God.

JUDAS   You are talking about setting up the arrest of Jesus?

LEVI   Yes. Our God is faithful. Never would it be permitted for the Messiah to suffer death. God would have to act. And in acting, all would see that Jesus is indeed the Christ. The people would rise, the Romans would be removed, and you and I would both have been unworthy servants in the bringing about of the reign of justice on this earth. Will you join me?

JUDAS   Yes. Yes, I will join you. It is true that God must act, for we cannot win without God's help. And Jesus would never be allowed to die. It must be as you say.

LEVI   And it must be done soon. You must not tell anyone of this plan. Come to me when Jesus is next in Jerusalem but alone, without all those crowds, and I will take care of everything else. We don't want to incite a rebellion, just do what is necessary. It is wonderful that we have a chance to be part of history, you and I.

JUDAS   For years I have dreamed of this time. God will act and all shall be revealed.

LEVI   Here is thirty pieces of silver for your coffers. It is only a small personal gift. Make sure that this Passover meal is the best ever, for it will be the last one before the people of Israel "pass over" for the last time.

JUDAS   You have surprised me, brother. I had not thought such faith existed within the priesthood of Israel.

LEVI   I am only hopeful that my God will see all that I have done and be grateful that I was an obedient servant.

JUDAS   Amen. Shalom.

LEVI   Shalom.

LEVI/LUCIFER sings "Satan Rules"; character takes off outer garments to reveal true identity.

During the song, the stage is set for the Last Supper Scene.

Scene 5

A table is set for the feast. Enter all disciples and followers, including the children, all celebrating Passover enthusiastically. JESUS wears the garment his mother gave him.

SARAH   Peter, you've had enough to drink; no more.

PETER   Quiet, it's Passover. Here (*to JOHN*), have another yourself.

JOHN   Thanks, Peter. (*to JESUS*) More wine?

JESUS   No, not now. In fact, I shall not drink wine again until I drink it in heaven with you all.

BVM   What do you mean?

MARTHA   Oh, he's just being poetic again. You know how he is.

JESUS   Yes, you know how I am. So how about this for poetry, Martha: This bread is my body, this wine, my blood. Like the bread and the wine, I will be broken for you, I will be poured out for you. Believe me when I tell you there is evil even here. Soon you will understand, so remember what I have just said, and remember this too.

Takes off outer garment and ties towel around waist. Begins to wash feet of all present. Continues through dialogue as long as necessary, but should finish by *.

ALL (*together*)   What are you doing? Why are you doing that now? What's going on?

JESUS goes to begin with PETER.

PETER   No, you're not going to wash my feet. It's not right.

JESUS   Peter, it's not about being right. It's about the poetry, right, Martha?

MARTHA   What do you mean?

JESUS   Peter, unless I wash your feet, you cannot be one of my disciples.

PETER   Then give me a bath!

SARAH   Peter!

JESUS   The feet are enough.

MARTHA   What do you mean, "poetry"?

JESUS   You all call me "Lord," "Teacher," "Master," and so I am. So, if I wash your feet, which is usually done by the least in the household, you should wash each other's. The Master is not greater than the servant. In my world, everyone is equal and the servant of the others. What I have done, you must do.

MARTHA   Strangest poetry I've ever heard.

JOHN   And?

JESUS   And what is done to me, will be done to you.

JOHN   Like broken bread and poured out wine?

JESUS   It's what you do for people when you love them.

MARTHA   John, why do you always understand what he says and the rest of never do!

JAMES   Because he's a poet too! My brother, the poet!

JOHN   And my brother, the realist!

SARAH   Your mother, God rest her soul, was right; she never got a moment's peace!

JOHN   The poet understands love.

JAMES   And the realist understands duty.

JESUS   And both are needed.

JAMES   But I don't see how you are the bread.

PETER   Or the wine.

JOHN (*to JESUS*)   Can I? See that over there? (*Points to whole loaf.*) What do you see?

JAMES   A loaf of bread.

JOHN   Do you feel nourished by seeing it?

JAMES   No, I feel hungry!

JOHN   Peter, what do you see here?

PETER   A bottle of lovely wine.

JOHN   And do you feel refreshed just by looking at it?

PETER   Not unless I drink it!

JOHN   Exactly. So if love is bread and wine, it has to be bread broken and shared, wine poured out and drunk. Otherwise we just look at it and know only the longing but never the fulfillment of the promise.

PETER   But what did you mean earlier when you said, "There's evil even here"?

* JESUS   John?

JOHN   Got me on that one.

MARTHA   At last!

JESUS   Then it is better for everyone to remain lost together, for no good will come out of naming evil tonight. Such things are best done in the light.

MARTHA   There he goes again!

JUDAS   I need to go and arrange a few things for tomorrow.

PETER   At this time of night?

JESUS   Go and do what you have to do, Judas. We are going to the Mount of Olives.

MALE DISCIPLES (*together*)   What? Now? At this time?

JESUS   We are going to the Mount of Olives to pray. Come on, the night air will do you good.

SARAH   Pray well, Peter. Or at least try and stay awake! (*Laughter; the disciples begin to exit but wait for JESUS.*)

BVM   Jesus, come here. (*She kisses him on the forehead. She puts his coat back on him.*) Pray for the deliverance of Israel and shalom for us all.

JESUS   I will.

All men exit.

MARTHA   Well, I suppose we better get this lot cleaned up and then get some sleep. Tomorrow will be here soon enough. Here, Mary, out of the daydream and help me with this.

ANNA (*to MARTHA*)   That sister of yours is in love with Jesus.

NAOMI   Quiet, Anna, she'll hear.

ANNA   I don't care if she hears. I think she's a nice girl, she'd make him a good wife, although he'd just be trouble as a husband, what with all this traveling around.

RUTH   Do you really think he might marry one of us?

SARAH   Don't expect it. If you ask me, being a prophet and teacher is a full time occupation.

MARTHA (*to her sister*)   What do you think Mary?

MARY   Pardon? What? Sorry, I was just thinking.

MIRIAM   She's a dreamer. She's always off somewhere, thinking. Your sister asked if you thought Jesus might marry one of you young girls.

MARY   I … I don't know. I'd like to be able to go with them tonight, and then go to the temple and the like.

RUTH   I think she wants to be a prophet herself.

NAOMI   And why not? Why can't all of us be prophets? We're all disciples.

ANNA   You're all in love with him; that's all this is about. (*They all stop and look at one another.*)

MARY   Love is one way of saying it, Anna, but it's not the only way.

NAOMI   And some of us are married, you might remember, so be careful what you say.

RUTH   But he's not.

MIRIAM   As one who knows about these things, believe me when I say JESUS is not the kind of man that can be loved enough by one person.

RUTH   What do you mean?

NAOMI   She means great men attract many admirers, and Jesus could never choose between his.

MARY   Nor should he have to. If I had to choose between marrying him and we being able to carry on like this, I think I would choose this.

ANNA   Miriam, why so quiet all of a sudden?

MIRIAM   You all know the story of how he and I met at the well in my old village. He knew my background, and yet he still talked with me. He's the first man in my life that didn't want something from me.

MARY   You love him for what he gave you. We all do I suppose, we've all been given so much.

ANNA   I still think one of you should marry him.

WOMEN (*together*)   Anna/ you never change/ give up/

SARAH   Don't you think it's time to settle down?

NAOMI   And dream?

RUTH   Dreams are fun.

MARY   Dreams are important.

MARTHA   Dreams are for dreamers!

Women settle for the night except MIRIAM.

MIRIAM sings "Beyond My Wildest Dreams."

At end, MIRIAM joins others, as if asleep. After time to settle, JOHN enters in a panic.

JOHN   Wake up, wake up! They've arrested Jesus; they've taken him away. Judas betrayed us; he's gone. Wake up. Mary, they've taken Jesus to the temple. It was a trick; they knew we were coming. There was nothing we could do.

MARTHA   Slow down. What are you talking about?

SARAH   Where's Peter; is he all right?

JOHN   We went to the garden to pray. Some of the men went to the homes where they are staying, the rest of us remained, but, one by one, fell asleep. And then they came—many of them, Romans as well as temple guards, I think. I'm not sure. Judas was with them. They only took Jesus. Peter wanted to fight them.

SARAH   Oh no!

JOHN   Jesus told him to stop, so he did.

BVM   John, what are they going to do with him?

JOHN   I don't know.

SARAH   What are we going to do?

BVM   We are going to go to the temple to pray. That is all we can do.

MIRIAM   That's not a good idea. Maybe we should stay here and wait to hear if it's safe.

BVM   At dawn, I will go the temple. If I am not safe there, I am safe nowhere.

All exit.

Scene 6

Enter JOSEPH of Arimathea and JOHN.

JOSEPH   I'm afraid it is no good. The Sanhedrin is totally in agreement with Annas and Caiaphas. They see it as necessary that one person should be sacrificed for the many.

JOHN   But no one needs to be sacrificed! Jesus hasn't done anything wrong.

JOSEPH   The priests are afraid that the zealots will attempt to make Jesus some sort of king.

JOHN   That's ridiculous! The zealots mock him; they say he has sold out to Judaism by befriending sinners and Gentiles. They are no more ready to make him king than make you or me emperor!

JOSEPH   Pilate doesn't see it that way. He holds the High Priest personally responsible for any actions of the guerrillas from the hills. Outlying garrisons have been attacked, and Pilate wants to know what we are going to do about it.

JOHN   What can you do?

JOSEPH   Nothing, which is why Caiaphas needs a sacrificial offering. And this way, he gets rid of any future challenge to the rule of the temple. You have to remember, Jesus has not made many friends here—but he has made enemies. When he arrived on a donkey last week, it made quite a stir. Jesus is not afraid of being noticed.

JOHN   Joseph, why are you a friend?

JOSEPH   Because, like you, I believe that, whoever he is and whatever God wants to do through him, Jesus is telling the truth. I cannot explain it anymore than that. He tells and does the truth. And I cannot deny that. I wish he were not so radical, so outspoken, so confrontational about things. But he is. Go and tell the disciples that it would be better to stay out of the way for the next little while. If this arrest pleases Pilate, there's no telling where it might stop.

JOHN   I'll tell them (*begins to exit*).

JOSEPH   And John, that goes for you too.

JOHN   I'll stay with Mary, but I won't abandon him.

JOSEPH   Then take care.

They exit in opposite directions. JOHN waits and joins BVM in next scene.

Scene 7

Note this entire scene is done very slowly and very quietly apart from the offstage piece and the final cry from JUDAS.

Music begins: "Officium" (from Scene 1). Crowd enters. JESUS, carrying crossbeam, and SOLDIERS thread their way through, to where BVM, WOMEN, and JOHN stand. They meet, but then JESUS gets moved on by the soldiers, and they exit through assembly to the back of the church.

The WOMAN from Scene 1 comes to BVM and they embrace.

Offstage sounds of hammering and cries.

Soundtrack dims.

From off stage:

SOLDIER 1   What about his tunic?

SOLDIER 2   That's a good one; looks like someone took some trouble with it.

SOLDIER 1   And it's nearly new.

SOLDIER 2   Shame about the blood though.

SOLDIER 1   Wanna throw for it? It's too good to cut up.

SOLDIER 2   What about the woman?

SOLDIER 1   She don't need it (*sound of dice being thrown*).

SOLDIER 1   Beat that (*dice thrown again*).

SOLDIER 2   Yes!

They re-enter through audience and walk back past the crowd, BVM and others exit, carrying the garment.

JUDAS enters and moves through the stationary crowd. He stops.

Organ music begins, low and quiet, with slow crescendo to complex, atonal explosion, and then silence.

All except JUDAS react as if they saw JESUS die, then silence and stillness.

JUDAS (*Looking around for signs of God coming in glory. Doesn't happen. Realizes he was tricked.*)   No! (*long scream*)

All exit slowly in silence, except JUDAS. Some go to cross, others off to sides. JUDAS is left alone. He drops the coins out of the bag as LUCIFER enters with hangman's noose. He drops one end in JUDAS' hands and leads him off.

Introduction begins to final song. Just a single note melody, very slowly, until all are in position. CAST re-enters as if gathering in an upper room, BVM is center, probably where JESUS was at the Passover meal. JOHN, PETER, and MIRIAM are near her.

BVM and MIRIAM, with JOHN, PETER, and ALL sing "There Can Be Miracles When You Believe."

A Holy Week Service Outline

PRESIDER   I greet you this evening in the name of our God,
        who loved us into being,
        who became one of us to find us and bring us home,
        and of the Spirit who continues to guide our steps and hearts. Amen.
        The Peace of Christ be with you all.

ALL   And also with you.

If this is the first time that a dramatized liturgy has been shared with the community, it might be appropriate to say a word of welcome and invitation to the new experience. However, do not feel you have to "explain" what is going to happen. Let the liturgy speak for itself.

PRESIDER   Once again we have gathered to remember the story of how Jesus our Brother
        and Lord loved us unto death.
         Let us be silent and pray.

Pause for shared silent reflection.

      Compassionate God,
      you who call your people to walk in the way of truth,
      the way of Jesus your Son,
      be here with us as we remember his passion and death,
      and the women and men who continue to make the choices he made.

      Open our hearts to the truth of your word;
      make it flesh in us,
      that we might answer the call to continue his witness to obedience in love;
      obedience even unto death.
      We make this prayer through the power of the life, death, and resurrection of Jesus
      the Christ, our Lord,

      Amen.

A reading might be shared here. Apart from biblical ones from the season, something such as the following excerpt from a homily by John Paul II might be appropriate for the plays in this book.*

      Like a cathedral, peace has to be constructed,
      patiently and with unshakable faith.
      Wherever the strong exploit the weak,

wherever the rich take advantage of the poor,
wherever great powers seek to dominate and to impose ideologies,
there the work of making peace is undone;
there the cathedral of peace is again destroyed.
The cathedral of peace is built of many small stones.
Each person has to become a stone in that beautiful edifice.
All people must deliberately and resolutely
commit themselves to the pursuit of peace.
Mistrust and division between nations begin
in the heart of the individual.
Work for peace starts when we listen to the urgent call of Christ:
"Repent and believe the Gospel."
We must turn from violence to peace,
we must turn from ourselves to Christ,
who alone can give us a new heart,
a new understanding.
We are living stones in the cathedral of peace.

Sung or silent response to the reading

The Passion Play

The play should begin without any special announcement or introduction. At the end of the play, if it is the local custom on that day, a veneration of the cross might take place. Otherwise it might be appropriate to give an extended time of silence before the intercessions.

Intercessions

PRESIDER   Called by the story of selfless love which we witness in Jesus the Christ,
and in the lives of all the women and men of the past, present, and future
who have or will die for their fidelity to others,
let us make our prayers to God.

Sung response

PRESIDER   Let us pray for this world, which is searching for meaning and truth,
for the whole of suffering humanity in this present age;
for all those who are the victims of war and racial or religious conflict,
for all those who are overwhelmed by natural disasters or the vastness of human
greed and selfishness.
We pray to the Lord.

Sung response

Let us pray for those who live in poverty, in destitution or without hope;
for those who despair and are depressed,
for the mentally ill and the physically challenged,
for those who live with ongoing illness and life-threatening disease.
We pray to the Lord.

Sung response

Let us pray for those who are searching for meaning in life;
for the young, who question the past,

and the old, who fear the future.
Let us pray for those who are questing for moral and inner strength to make right choices;
for us, when we are faced with the temptation to deny the truth for convenience or personal gain.
We pray to the Lord.

Sung response

Let us pray for the people of this parish, this city, this state;
for tolerance and understanding,
for community and friendship,
for unity without uniformity,
and for trust in goodwill.
We pray to the Lord.

Sung response

Let us pray for the visitors and strangers in our midst,
for the political refugees and the economic orphans,
for families split apart and for migrant or sweatshop workers in every country who are denied justice and fair treatment.
Let us pray for the martyrs of every age and place,
whose blood still calls us to perseverance and obedience, even unto death.
We pray to the Lord.

Sung response

God of history and truth,
we behold you in the broken body of Jesus our Brother
and in the broken lives of those who surround us.
Let not this story be for nothing.
Let us hear with hearts of flesh the call to be strong in faithfulness and love;
inspire us to work for justice and peace
in the many areas of pain that daily touch our lives.

We make this prayer in the power of the life, death, and resurrection of the One who came to show us the true meaning of love, Jesus Christ, our Brother, who lives with you in the power of your Holy Spirit,
God, for ever and ever.
Amen.

Invitation to the Lord's Prayer

Blessing and Dismissal [optional]

Final song

*SOURCE: The suggested reading is extracted from a homily by John Paul II found in *Celebrating One World*, CAFOD and St. Thomas More Centre (London: 1989).

Music Suggestions and Sources

The music in each play makes a huge difference to the experience of the assembly. However, given that every community is not necessarily blessed with an experienced choir or other singers, it is important to remember that it might be better not to have live music if the standard is not on a par with the rest of the production. In some situations, recordings can be used, and the cast can sing along, or, more likely, the popular music can be replaced with community hymns and songs. Alternatively, instrumental pieces could be played, live or recorded. Indeed, sometimes it might be possible to leave out the music all together. I hope directors will be realistic about what can be achieved while maintaining the overall effectiveness of the liturgies and use the community's talents to their best advantage. With the developments in music production technology, this might be one area into which to invite the more computer-literate members of the community, who otherwise do not find a place on the worship or catechetics teams.

Because of copyright costs and difficulties in tracing some copyright owners, we were not able to print the music or lyrics to the songs in this publication. We hope this does not diminish your interest in producing the scripts as originally conceived. To this end, I have endeavored to provide as detailed a record as possible of the music originally used for the liturgies. If you have difficulty finding some pieces, try anthologies from different years and styles of music, including wonderful sources such as *The Ultimate Fake Book* series, especially *The Ultimate Broadway Fake Book*. While most of the songs taken from shows have recordings in ready supply, I have given details of other recordings where I have them. Again, the internet might prove a valuable resource. Please remember that photocopying is a serious infringement of the owners' copyright. But if the pieces are being used in a service and no fee is charged to the people, making the assembly an "audience," there is usually no fee to be paid for use of the music. However, be sure to check with the copyright holder to be certain.

Mention is made below and in the individual scripts about necessary word changes in some songs. Please read all the lyrics to songs you choose. Extra word changes, and even deleting extra verses, might be necessary because the edition you find is different from that used for the original productions. Note should also be taken that the popular styling of songs, often with what are called "vocal licks" (or, more accurately, "grace notes"), does not transfer well to the liturgical setting or biblical character styling. Musical directors are encouraged to work with individual singers and the choruses to make all such individualization of songs appropriate to the overall service.

Please note you may wish to transfer and interchange some pieces between plays. Indeed, other music you know or write could replace the following selections. I have included some other ideas and suggestions at the end of this chapter.

Music is given in the order it appears in the plays.

The Advent Plays

"Glory Be!"

Hamlisch, Marvin, and Edward Kleban. **"One."** *A Chorus Line*. Wren Music Co., and American Music Corp., 1975. Use only the main refrain, changing pronouns and related words to "we," "we're," and so forth, as necessary for the opening number, and then to "she" or "he" versions in the annunciation scene.

Sondheim, Stephen. **"The Hills of Tomorrow."** *Merrily We Roll Along*. Revelation Music Publishing Corp. and Rilting Music Inc., 1981.

Batt, Mike. **"I Watch You Sleeping."** Recorded by John Denver on *The Flower That Shattered the Stone*. Belfry Prod., 1988.

Hamlisch, Marvin, and Edward Kleban. **"Sing."** *A Chorus Line*. Wren Music Co. and American Music Corp., 1975.

Hamlisch, Marvin, and Edward Kleban. **"Let Me Dance For You."** *A Chorus Line*. Wren Music Co. and American Music Corp., 1975. Use as much or as little of this number as your singer(s)/dancer(s) need to create the image of a strong "song and dance" routine.

Mann, Barry, Cynthia Weil, and Tom Snow. **"Don't Know Much (But I Know I Love You)."** Recorded by Linda Ronstadt and Arron Neville on *Cry Like a Rainstorm, Howl Like the Wind*. ATV Music, Mann & Weil Songs, Inc., Snow Music, and Braintree Music, 1980.

Porter, Cole. **"Blow, Gabriel, Blow."** *Anything Goes*. Warner Bros. Inc., 1934.

"Celestial Secrets"

Hamlisch, Marvin, and Edward Kleban. **"One."** *A Chorus Line*. Wren Music Co. and American Music Corp., 1975.

Black, Don, and Elmer Bernstein. **"Something More."** *Merlin*. London: Dick James Music Ltd., 1983.

Herman, Jerry. **"The Man in the Moon."** *Mame*. Jerryco Music Co., 1966.

Denver, John. **"The Gift You Are."** *The Flower That Shattered the Stone*. Cherry Mountain Music (ASCAP), 1989.

Black, Don, and Elmer Bernstein. **"He Who Knows The Way."** *Merlin*. London: Dick James Music Ltd., 1983.

Harburg, E.Y., and Burton Lane. **"That Great Come and Get It Day."** *Finian's Rainbow*. Chappel & Co. Inc., 1946.

"Paradise Lost and Found"

Merrill, Bob, and Jule Styne. **"The Music That Makes Me Dance."** *Funny Girl*. Bob Merrill & Jule Styne, 1963 and 1964.

"Holy, Holy, Holy." I suggest using any (short) setting of this acclamation, traditional or modern, that is well known by the cast and assembly.

Hamlisch, Marvin, and Edward Kleban. **"One."** *A Chorus Line*. Wren Music Co. and American Music Corp., 1975. Change the pronouns to "you," "you're," and so forth.

Herman, Jerry. **"Wherever He Ain't."** *Mack and Mabel*. Jerryco Music Co., 1974. Note that the "He" of the title is God in this script, and therefore the pronoun should be varied to reflect the gender(s) of the person(s) playing that part. The name "God" can also be used as a variant. The "seven years" mentioned in the opening verse (which should be included) should become "seven days." And, of course, the name of the singer has to change from "Mabel" to "Lucifer."

Merrill, Bob, and Jule Styne. **"You Are Woman, I Am Man."** *Funny Girl*. Bob Merrill & Jule Styne, 1963 and 1964.

Bock, Jerry, and Sheldon Harnick. **"The Apple Tree."** *The Apple Tree*. Recorded by Matt Munro. Appletree Music Co. and Carlin Music Co., 1966.

Anderson, Maxwell, and Kurt Weill. **"Lost in the Stars."** *Lost in the Stars*. New York: Hampshire House Publishing Corp. and Chappell & Co., Inc., 1944 and 1946.

Gershwin, George. **"Stairway to Paradise."** WB Music Corp., 1922.

"A Family Christmas Tradition"

Carols

"**This Little Light of Mine**" (traditional spiritual). *Lead Me, Guide Me*. GIA Publications.

Lillis, OSC, Eileen. "**Christ the Light Is Coming.**" *Breaking Bread*. OCP Publications, 1965. No. 48.

Wesley, John, and Christian Witt. "**Come Thou Long Expected Jesus.**" *Breaking Bread*.
   OCP Publications, 1998. No. 41.

"**Creator of the Starry Sky**" (traditional) (also published as "Creator of the Stars of Night").
   The Church Pension Fund, 1985. (Also found in *Breaking Bread*. OCP Publications, 1985. No. 50.)

Tate, Nathum, and George Handel. "**While Shepherds Watched Their Flocks**" (traditional).
   Breaking Bread. OCP Publications, 1998. No. 89.

Brownlie, John, and John Wyeth. "**The King Shall Come.**" *Lead Me, Guide Me*. GIA Publications.

Farrell, Bernadette. "**Christ Be Our Light.**" OCP Publications, 1994. (Also found in *Breaking Bread*.
   OCP Publications, 1998. No. 460.)

Haugen, Marty. "**Carol at the Manger.**" 1987. (Also found in *Gather*. GIA Publications, 1988. No. 152.)

Songs

Merrill, Bob, and Jule Styne. "**I'm The Greatest Star.**" *Funny Girl*. Bob Merrill & Jule Styne,
   1963 and 1964.

Koffman, Moe, Rhoda Roberts, and Kenny Jacobson. "**The Swinging Shepherd Blues.**" New York:
   NOM MUSIC, INC., 1958.

Keith, Barbara. "**Free the People.**" Recorded by Delaney & Bonnie and Friends, ATCO Records.
   New York: Leo Feist, Inc., 1970.

The Passion Plays

"No Greater Love"

Denver, John, John Christopher, Sam Hogin, and Conrad Reeder. "**Thanks to You.**" Recorded by
   John Denver on *The Flower That Shattered the Stone*. Cherry Mountain Music, 1989.

Denver, John, and Joe Henry. "**Eagles and Horses (I'm Flying Again).**" Recorded by John Denver on
   The Flower That Shattered the Stone. Cherry Mountain Music, 1989.

Bonoff, Karla. "**Goodbye My Friend.**" Recorded by Linda Ronstadt on *Cry Like a Rainstorm, Howl Like
   the Wind*. Seagrape Music (BMI), 1988.

Black, Don, and Andrew Lloyd Webber. "**Unexpected Song.**" *Song and Dance*. The Really Useful
   Company Ltd., Dick James Music Ltd., and Chappell Music Ltd., 1981. Various recordings.

"**The Angel Gabriel**" (traditional Basque carol).

Webb, Jimmy. "**Shattered.**" Recorded by Linda Ronstadt on *Cry Like a Rainstorm, Howl Like the Wind*.
   Seagrape Music (BMI), 1981.

Denver, John. "**The Flower That Shattered the Stone.**" Cherry Mountain Music, 1989.

"God of The Outcasts"

Bergman, Alan, Marilyn Bergman, and Michel Legrand. "**Papa Can You Hear Me?**" *Yentl*. Emanuel Music
   and Threesome Music Co., 1983.

Margoshes, Levy; Christopher Gore; and Michael Gore. "**Out Here on My Own.**" *Fame*. MGM/United
   Artists, 1980.

"**Dies Ire**" from the *Verdi Requiem*. Use a recording, and only use as much as you need, not the whole
   piece.

Samuels, J. "**Shelter of Your Arms.**" Recorded by Neil Diamond on *September Morn*. CBS Inc., 1979.

King, Carole. "**Being at War with Each Other.**" Recorded by Barbra Streisand. Colgems-AMI Music Inc.,
   1973.

Sondheim, Stephen. **"Not a Day Goes By."** *Merrily We Roll Along*. Revelation Music Publishing Corp. and Rilting Music Inc., 1981. Use only the main verse, as per the version sung by Bernadette Peters in the recording *Stephen Sondheim: A Celebration at Carnegie Hall*.

"Come to My House"

Townshend, Pete. **"Come to My House"** (recorded as "Welcome"). *Tommy*. Fabulous Music Ltd., 1969 and 1975.

Menken, Alan, and Stephen Schwartz. **"God Help the Outcasts."** *The Hunchback of Notre Dame*. Wonderland Music and Walt Disney Music, 1996.

McCartney, Paul. **"Daytime Nighttime Suffering."** MPL Communications Ltd., 1979. (Also published in *Paul McCartney: Composer/Artist*, distributed by Simon and Shuster.)

Crossman, Samuel, and John Ireland. **"My Song Is Love Unknown."** *Breaking Bread*. OCP Publications, 1998. No. 405.

Menken, Alan, and Stephen Schwartz. **"Someday."** *The Hunchback of Notre Dame*. Wonderland Music and Walt Disney Music, 1996.

"Weaving Between Heaven and Earth"

Garbarek, Jan, and The Hilliard Ensemble. **"Officium."** Track one, *Parce mihi Domini*. ECM New Series. ECM Records, 1993.

A Psalm. I suggest a joyous one with a strong Jewish folk rhythm, such as Marty Haugen's setting of Psalm 16, **"You Will Show Me the Path of Life,"** published by GIA Publications.

Schönberg, Claude-Michael, and Alain Boublil. **"I'd Give My Life For You."** *Miss Saigon*. Alain Boublil Music Ltd., 1987.

Black, Don, and Elmer Bernstein. **"Satan Rules."** *Merlin*. Dick James Music Ltd., 1983 (as in *The Ultimate Broadway Fake Book*).

Black, Don, and Elmer Bernstein. **"Beyond My Wildest Dreams."** *Merlin*. Dick James Music Ltd., 1983 (as in *The Ultimate Broadway Fake Book*). Suggest reducing the accompaniment to a minimum, without the original waltz energy, making it more ballad-like.

Zimmer, Hans, and Stephen Schwartz. **"(There Can Be Miracles) When You Believe."** *The Prince of Egypt*. Dream Works SKG, 1998. Use the main theme's verses and refrain only; do not use the Hebraic chant.

Other Selections

Babyface, and L.A. Reid. "Miracle." Epic/Solar Songs Inc. & Kear Music Epic/Solar Songs Inc., 1990 and 1991.

Bergman, Alan; Marilyn Bergman; and Michel Legrand. **"On My Way to You."** Recorded by Barbra Streisand. Threesome Music Ltd., 1988.

Curtis, Mann; Pierre DeLanoe; and Gilbert Becaud. **"Let It Be Me."** Recorded by Willie Nelson. New York: France Music Co., 1955, 1957, and 1960.

Denver, John. **"Perhaps Love."** Recorded by John Denver and Placido Domingo. Cherry Lane Music Publishing Co., 1980. Yeston, Maury. **"Till I Loved You."** *Goya*. Yeston Music Ltd., 1987.

Rich, Allan; James Newton Howard; and Jud Friedman. **"For the First Time."** *One Fine Day*. Recorded by Kenny Loggins. MCA Music Publishing/Universal Studios, 1996.

Sondheim, Stephen. **"Children Will Listen."** *Into the Woods*. Rilting Music Inc., 1988.

Warren, Diane. **"Because You Loved Me."** *Up Close and Personal*. Recorded by Celine Dion. Realsongs, 1996.

Webber, Andrew Lloyd. **"Love Changes Everything."** *Aspects of Love*. The Really Useful Music Co., 1988.

Yeston, Maury. **"Till I Loved You."** *Goya*. Yeston Music Ltd., 1987.